Why Would I Want the Toy, When I Can Have the Box?

Quality /2.95

W9-BDX-137

159331

Why Would I Want the Toy, When I Can Have the Box?

101 Ways to Make the Most of Your Children, With the Least from Your Wallet

FOR PARENTS WITH CHILDREN AGES 3-6

BY REX BOWLBY

ILLUSTRATIONS BY LEILA CABIB

PACIFIC HORIZON PRESS

Shelbyville-Shelby County
Public Library

Copyright © 2000 by Rex Bowlby

Illustrations Copyright © 2000 by Leila Cabib

All rights reserved. No part of this book may be reproduced or transmitted in any form or by any means, electronic or mechanical, including photo-copying, recording, or by any information storage and retrieval system, without permission in writing from the publisher.

Published by Pacific Horizon Press
1025 Rose Creek Drive, 620-372
Woodstock, GA 30189

Cover Design by Robert Aulicino
Cover Illustrations by Leila Cabib

Publisher's Cataloging-in-Publication
(Provided by Quality Books, Inc.)

Bowlby, Rex
    Why would I want the toy, when I can have the box? : 101 ways to make the most of your children, with the least from your wallet / Rex Bowlby ; illustrations by Leila Cabib. — 1st ed.

    p. cm.
    Includes index.
    LCCN: 99-63562
    ISBN: 0-9672496-3-5

    1. Parenting. 2. Child-rearing 3. Fatherhood — Anecdotes. I. Cabib, Leila. II. Title.

HQ755.8.B69 2000   649'.5
                                                         QBI00-50

The purpose of this book is to educate and entertain. Nevertheless, all the activities herein should be conducted with appropriate adult supervision. Due care should be exercised by parents and/or guardians in selection of activities, especially with regard to age appropriateness of the activity. The author and Pacific Horizon Press shall be in no way liable for any adverse actions or mishaps arising directly or indirectly from inadequately supervised activities, or from adverse actions or mishaps arising from instructions included in any part of this book. If you do not wish to be bound by the above, you may return this book to the publisher for a full refund.

Printed in the United States of America
First Edition
10 9 8 7 6 5 4 3 2 1

To my parents,
who taught me to think outside the box

and

To my children,
who taught me to play inside the box

ACKNOWLEDGMENTS

With much appreciation to the following: David Bernardi, Bobbie Christmas, Cindy Kennett, and Carl Nelson, for their sharp eyes and even sharper pencils. David Baker for his mark. Dan Poynter for his spark. My wife Barbara for her encouragement, wisdom, and tact. Ryan and Eric who showed me the boxes, and who agreed the illustrations should include a girl, because the boxes are for girls, too. Marion Singleton for her long-ago praise. Leila Cabib and Bob Aulicino for their high standards. Leo and LaVonne who provided the raw materials, and Hugh Bowlby, Margaret Bowlby Mercer, and Charles Mercer, who manufactured the product. The many publishers, parents, and toy makers that provided the polarity. The day job that provided the time and lessons. And Mother Nature for her hard work, quiet way, and perseverance.

CONTENTS

If I had to live my life over
I would have sat on the lawn with my children
and not worried about the grass stains

Erma Bombeck

INTRODUCTION

What's Wrong with This Picture?

I knew my son's third birthday was going to be a great one. Why? I had bought him the present to end all presents, a spaceship that had it all: flashing and spinning colored lights, computer sounds, multiple buttons, and motorized doors. It was expensive, but it didn't matter. He opened up the box, and I inserted enough batteries to power a small city. The toy lit up like a row of searchlights, and so did my son's eyes. I patted myself on the back and went about my business.

Later that day, I heard my son excitingly calling me from downstairs, "Daddy, come here, look!" *Most of the day had passed and he was still playing with that spaceship. Was there any better dad than me?* When I got halfway down the stairs, I spotted the shiny spaceship—however, it was nowhere near my son. No, he was on the other side of the room, stretched out, coloring on *the box* the spaceship had come in. "Daddy look! I made a robot head. Watch." He placed the box on his head. A simply drawn purple face covered the box.

Something was wrong with this picture—no, not the one on the box, the one taking place in the room. Why would my apparently normal son choose to play with a box, instead of, well, the best toy from the finest dad? "Here, let's put a couple of holes in it for the eyes," I suggested. This curious irony deserved some examination.

I recalled the previous Christmas, most of the toys saw daylight for little more than a day before they came to a permanent rest under a bed, in a closet, or behind a piece of living room furniture. "Hey, Son, let's see if we can find some cardboard cylinders left over from paper towels and toilet paper, and make some antennas and a nose." So if my son wasn't playing with toys, then just what was he playing with, and why? The answer to that question, and its many aspects, is what this book is about.

Thinking Outside the Box

I might have explained away the spaceship-box incident as an aberration, a result of misguided parenting or poor gene pool. Such an easy explanation, however, was difficult to accept, because I observed such choices on a regular basis, initially with my first child and subsequently with my second child. There had to be more to this behavior than met the eye.

Conventional children's toys and games were being displaced by a variety of quasi-activities that appeared trivial and meaningless, yet my children's smiles were bigger, their attention spans greater, and my wallet healthier. Hmmmm? Nevertheless, was this frivolous play—play that was in most cases selected by my offspring—supplanting the get-down, roll-up-your-sleeves, serious-mindedness, of raising children? Since my psychology education didn't include any fathering or parenting classes, I didn't have a clue.

Nonetheless, I observed that my children and I were playing together, physically interacting, and bonding a great deal. I also noticed that most activities were not gender based, and could be tied to some fundamental area of child development. Child development? Bonding? That sounds pretty serious-minded, doesn't it?

Although my children's behavior was unconventional, paradoxically, it seemed very natural. That's it! Natural—NATURE! Wouldn't Mother Nature have programmed our children for success, realizing as we go, so she goes? Could it ironically be that children, not parents, or capitalists in the name of toy and game makers, have the inside track on purposeful play? After all, it is tough to question the skill and motives of Mother Nature.

Well, it's my theory that children *are* guided by her, and if we observe and exploit our children's natures, we all will have a leg up.

This book chronicles, by way of 101 illustrations of play organized into 13 categories of development, how such an approach came to pass in our household.

What I Think Mother Nature Had in Mind

Although I hesitate to put words into her mouth, I believe Mother Nature had development plans in her quest for our children's success. I have based the book's 13 chapters on what might be Mother Nature's Plans.

Chapter 1. CONTRIBUTING to chores to acquire *self-confidence.*
Chapter 2. Investigating the ADULT WORLD to secure *knowledge.*
Chapter 3. Playing *make-believe* to develop IMAGINATION.
Chapter 4. Pursuing AEROBIC ACTIVITY to become *fit and healthy.*
Chapter 5. Asking about FAMILY ROOTS to gain a sense of *belonging.*
Chapter 6. Seeking *closeness* to establish a BONDING.
Chapter 7. *Making* things to increase CREATIVITY.
Chapter 8. Exploring the *ecology* to attain an appreciation of NATURE.
Chapter 9. *Performing* to get comfortable with EXPRESSION.
Chapter 10. *Guessing and solving* to procure INTELLECT.
Chapter 11. Executing *physical challenges* to obtain COORDINATION.
Chapter 12. Exercising the RELEASE VALVE to achieve good *mental health.*
Chapter 13. Receiving POSITIVE REINFORCEMENT to realize *self-esteem.*

The Vehicles

Here is a glimpse at some of the activities contained in this book and their potential for fun, cost-free play, and development.

Find out HOW:

- A box of scrap wood can be a great ally when *you* want to get things done (p. 24).
- A child's potty time is a perfect bonding time (p. 81).
- A tape recorder can quickly extinguish a sibling squabble (p. 115).
- A plain deck of cards can provide many fundamental learning opportunities (p. 122).
- A car parking aid in the garage doubles as a multi-purpose sports device (p. 127).

Find out WHY:

- Dishwashers are a step backwards (p. 21).
- Hiring a gardener would be a mistake (pp. 22 and 27).
- Baking is more than just a lesson in home economics (p. 23).
- Supermarkets (p. 33), and hair salons (p. 142), serve another purpose.
- Pencil and paper will someday be a new discovery (p. 101).

Find out HOW:

- Water can encourage imagination (p. 47) and aerobic activity (p. 62).
- Socks promote imagination (p. 49) and double as a release valve (p. 139).
- Storage rooms bring the family together (p. 69).
- Driving in the rain can be a learning adventure (p. 106).
- Shaving cream fosters creativity and defuses tension (p. 137).

From the Heart of a Father

I wrote *Why Would I Want the Toy, When I Can Have the Box?* because I acquired a different perspective on parenting, one that doesn't suppose parents have to approach parenting the way a doctoral candidate approaches a thesis; one that doesn't suggest the key to parenting is elusive and buried deep within the ground or the psyche.

Instead, the book suggests the key to parenting is nestled in our children's hands, within arm's length of each parent. It proposes that the best solutions, even to complex tasks such as parenting, are often the simplest solutions. This work is written in this spirit—a spirit containing much irony.

Maybe the best way to sum up this work is by way of contrast. It is NOT:

- A telling book, but a showing book.
- A scientific book, but an artistic book.
- An instruction book, but an entertaining book.
- A book fully from an adult's point of view, but one equally from a child's perspective.
- A book that bounds like a straight jacket, but offers freedom of motion like a loose suit.
- An intellectual book that plays on paper, but a practical book that plays in real life.
- A book of prose from the brain of a scholar, but anecdotes from the heart of a father.

It is also not a by-the-numbers cookbook-type activity book either, but a spontaneous and free-form book. To classify this work as just another activity book is analogous to suggesting *The Wizard of Oz* is just another movie with a dream sequence.

The intent of this book is not for you to mimic each activity as related. Every family is different; consequently, each must travel its own road to success. View this book as a framework, to observe your children, and capitalize on their nature with the hope that *your* version of this book will emerge.

Then, on the next gift-giving occasion when your children open a toy and look at you with confused expressions, you'll know it isn't because they don't know what the toy is or does, but because they are trying to tell you, "Why would I want the toy, when I can have the box?"

1

CONTRIBUTING

- *Washing the Dishes*

- *Scrap Wood Projects*

- *Trimming the Bushes*

- *Lawn Mowers*

- *Washing the Car*

- *Bathing the Dog*

- *Baking*

- *Cleanup*

Children want desperately to please their parents, although it is often difficult to recognize. They want to contribute and do something meaningful, but where do they start? They want to emulate their parents, however questionable that desire might be. And if enthusiasm were the only prerequisite to realize these aspirations, then our children would have the world by the tail—but it isn't, and they don't because, well, they're children.

When your children plead to help you with a chore or project, often your reflex response is a firm "NO." They ask, "Why?" You say, "Because you will hurt yourself," or "Because you don't know how," or "Because we don't have the time," or "Because I don't want to have to do it over again."

I say to you: Supervise them, so they won't hurt themselves. Teach them, so they will know how. Time is artificial and restrictive; there is *always* time for something important. And does it have to be done perfectly?

True, you will make some obvious minor sacrifices, but by not allowing children to contribute means you will be making some not so obvious—major sacrifices. The children lose out on being challenged, learning from mistakes, succeeding at a task, and building self-esteem. You lose out by missing the opportunity to learn patience, to get some free assistance, and to gain pride—the pride you get by watching your child wanting to please you and be like you.

. . . Just another one of life's cruel little paradoxes.

1. Washing the Dishes   *"Life's Cruel Paradox"*

Aunt Bea is washing. Andy is drying. A trivial problem is being discussed and pondered at about the same slow pace as the dishes move from hand to hand over the kitchen sink.

With the introduction of the dishwasher, the family communication that often took place while doing the dishes has all but disappeared. So much for progress. Nevertheless, there is another way to realize a gain from this ostensibly mundane chore. Have your child *do* the dishes. Yes, I said DO, not clean. To suggest otherwise would only be leading you down the primrose path.

Think about it. Washing the dishes includes the following attractive elements for children: water, soapy bubbles, spray-hose, sponge, brush, and of course—mess. So it is just a matter of time before your children's curiosity kicks in and the nagging begins. Let's look at some of the trade-offs.

CON: It personifies the axiom, "An accident waiting to happen."
PRO: It will hold their attention for quite a long time.

CON: It's like Russian roulette, except you stand a better chance in roulette.
PRO: They feel as if they are making a contribution to the household.

CON: This was Murphy's inspiration for *his* law.
PRO: It will encourage them to volunteer for other chores.

CON: A good portion of the water ends up on the floor.
PRO: The water on the floor gives you a good start toward mopping it.

As you can see, this task is just another one of life's cruel little paradoxes: When children are too young to be productive, they want to help, and when they are old enough to be productive, they of course—don't. Despite the overwhelming potential for disaster, it's worth it just to see them standing on a chair with eyes of determination, extended tongue of concentration, a will to succeed, and all the while losing ground. Then, when they say they are done, *you* put the dishes in the dishwasher, clean up *their* mess, pat them on the back, and tell them, "great job."

2. Lawn Mowers   *"The Three Musketeers"*

A neighborhood boy mowed my lawn one summer, 5,000 square feet of it, at $30 a pop. Since mowing took virtually a half day out of my weekend with the children, hiring someone else to do it seemed like a wonderful idea. Right? Wrong. What I did was take away from the children one of their most enjoyable pleasures and took away from my wife and me an enjoyable $30 dinner out.

So what made this mowing chore so attractive to the children? I guess if I were a young child and witnessed the following, I would better understand.

Daddy funnels a strong-smelling liquid from a fire-red container (gas can) into another fire-red object (the lawn mower). He pulls hard on a rope, multiple times, to ignite a fierce roar, accompanied by smoke. He pulls and pushes on a lever that makes the roar louder and then softer. He pushes this large roaring machine around. As he does, the grass appears to disappear inside of it. He stops the machine and takes the bag off in the back. It contains sweet-smelling green bits. He dumps the grass into the mulch pile and starts again.

Fire-red machine, pulling a rope, loud roar, pushing, dumping! What a surprise that they want to be involved in this activity. And they are, from the moment I yank the rope to the moment when the roar stops. One child on each side of me, like The Three Musketeers. Our oversized safety glasses make us look as if we stepped out of a bad science fiction movie.

For half a day, every week or two, we parade around together. Not a toy in the world has held their attention for that long, and it doesn't change from week to week, month to month, and so far, year to year. They never tire of it or get bored with it.

Then often, a day or two after the lawn has been mowed, my oldest child, figuring that I wouldn't notice the lawn hasn't grown, suggests, "Dad, I think it's time to push the red machine across the grass again."

3. Baking *"More Than Meets the Eye"*

Today your children will learn mathematics, decision making, direction following, task distribution, and gratification delay. For 10 points, which activity will they be participating in?

A. First day in Corporate America   C. First day in the Armed Services
B. First day at the University   D. Baking

If you chose A, B, or C, you might have been right, except your child is only five years old. So how about D?

What appears to be only a labor-intensive task of messiness, tedium, and frazzled nerves, also packs a punch when it comes to indirect learning. Here's a sampling of the curriculum:

DECISION MAKING: Cake, cookies, or brownies (OK, brownies it is) ✦ Pillsbury, Betty Crocker, or Duncan Hines ✦ Frosted, nuts, or "original" recipe ✦ Fudge-like, cake-like, no-cholesterol, or extra-thick ✦ Metal, plastic, or glass bowl ✦ Deep, wide, or large bowl ✦ Plastic, metal, or wooden spoon ✦ Round, square, or rectangular pan . . . (*"Enough already, we get the idea!"*)

MATHEMATICS: Temperature (350 degrees) ✦ Time (24-26 minutes baking; 20 minutes cooling) ✦ Volume (1/4 cup water; 1/2 cup oil) ✦ Area (pan 13x9x2) ✦ High-altitude cooking (3,500-6,500 feet) ✦ Weight (2 grams of fat; 28 grams of carbohydrate) ✦ Percent of daily value (2% Niacin; 13% fat) ✦ Whole numbers (50 strokes) ✦ Monetary ($1.19/box)

DIRECTION FOLLOWING: (If you don't think it is necessary to follow directions, just try to grease the pan *after* pouring in the ingredients!)

TASK DISTRIBUTION: (Between siblings or between parent and child) ✦ Getting the ingredients or putting them away ✦ Measuring out or pouring in ✦ Stirring bowl or pouring into pan ✦ Greasing pan or washing pan ✦ Setting timer or putting in oven ✦ Taste testing batter or licking the bowl ✦ Cleaning counter or utensils ✦ If dissatisfied with the results: One does the dialing to the toll free number, and the other talks.

GRATIFICATION DELAY: Does switching on the oven light speed up baking? ✦ Does opening the oven numerous times shorten baking time? ✦ Does eating up the raw batter make for more of the finished product? ✦ Does blowing on the finished brownies speed up cooling time? You get the idea.

It probably goes without saying, that if one of your vivid childhood memories is of kitchen warmth and aromas, while baking and bonding with Mom, then chances are you succeeded in any or all of A, B, and C.

4. Scrap Wood Projects   *"Win-Win Situation"*

Homo sapiens has built, constructed, and assembled, ever since the first sapien attempted putting together two rocks with his phlegm. The powerful inborn trait first shows itself when children watch Dad build something with tools. This translates into a strong desire to participate, which leaves you with a decision to make: Do I want to have a stereo cabinet, or do I want to have happy, well-adjusted children? Well, you can have your cake and eat it too.

Gather up all the small pieces of scrap wood—boards and miscellaneous lumber—lying around. (Since you are such a handy guy, you should have plenty.) Lay them down in front of your children and explain that you want them to help you build the "framistan," which is the most important part of the stereo cabinet.

They will beam with delight, tickled that you would include them in such important matters. Give them a small tool box with a hammer, nails, screwdriver, screws, nuts, bolts, wrench, saw, file, glue, sandpaper, and paint, and then watch their expressions go from tickled to ecstatic. NOW, you can alternate between completing your project and helping them with theirs. It might go something like this:

1.   Help them saw three or four pieces of wood, then let them sand and file the rough edges.
2.   Help them drill a hole and start a screw for them, then let them work the screwdriver.
3.   Have them apply some glue (which they will be very adept at; you can be assured they won't scrimp).
4.   Help them hammer the nails.
5.   Help them drill some large holes, supply them with bolts and nuts, and let them turn the wrench.
6.   Give them a brush and paint to finish off—as you will tell them—the most terrific framistan ever made.

While my children and I stood back and admired the projects we had completed, I smugly gloated at the win-win situation I had created, until my oldest child asked, "Which part of the stereo cabinet does the *famifam* go into?"

I, of course, panicked, fearful I would have to look at it every time I watched television. Fortunately, my spouse stepped in and calmly told him, "The framistan goes in *the back* . . . to help organize all the cords." Whew.

5. Washing the Car   *"It's the Means"*

Are you stuck for something to do on a hot summer day? The children are champing at the bit, eager to work off their boundless energy, while you want to park your bottom somewhere and make progress toward completion of that novel.

There is a solution. Issue one regulation bucket of soapy water and a sponge to one child, and a hose with slow running water to the other. (If you have more or less than two children, you can improvise.) Point them in the direction of the family vehicle, then nestle into the lawn chair and commence reading. You may ask, "How can young children who cannot reach much of the automobile do any kind of an effective job?" The answer is: Go back and start over. You missed the whole point. Never mind, I'll summarize. They work off *their* energy and you save *yours*. It's the means, and not the end, that's important.

Although you are able to stay seated, you won't end up making much progress on your novel, though. The *Our Gang* comedy feature unfolding before you is much more entertaining.

My youngest child washes the tires because they are black—therefore dirty. My oldest child, very logically, washes the door handles over and over because, "They always get touched." My oldest tells the youngest, "Rinse that dirty spot with the hose so I don't get my sponge dirty." Before it's all over, both kids are soaked, squealing, and chasing each other with hose and bucket. I generally get my dose of water, even though I'm always explicit about Daddy being "off limits." Which is why I'm always wet—they have no idea of what off limits means.

When the children are finished (yes, it is hard to tell), we all get in the car and head to the drive-through car wash, all except for Mom. She volunteers to stay home and dry out Dad's water-soaked novel with her hair dryer.

Shelbyville-Shelby County
Public Library

6. Cleanup   *"When Life Gives You Lemons . . ."*

"This hardly qualifies as an activity; in fact, I'd call it just plain drudgery," you say. I say, you only have three choices here, so pick one.

- Never clean up. (I don't know anybody who has ever tried this, so I can't honestly report on the results.)

- Continue with the status quo. Use the "bang your head against the wall" approach in trying to get your children to clean up after themselves. Do any of the following methods sound familiar?

  1. SARCASM: "I'm glad we bought a $400 recliner to hold your dirty socks."
  2. PSYCHOLOGY: "If you don't go to bed on time, you *can't* clean up tomorrow."
  3. LOGIC: "Put it back in its place, so you know where it is next time."
  4. SYMPATHY: "I didn't clean up as a child, because I had nothing to clean up."
  5. THREAT: "These toys would be perfect to stoke up a dying fire."
  6. SCARE: "Yeah, that's right, spiders love to crawl into unmade beds."
  7. HUMOR: "If you didn't get your toys out, they must be trying to escape."
  8. PROVERBS: "A place for everything and everything in its place."
  9. LYING: "When I was little, cleaning up was my favorite thing to do."
  10. REWARD: "You'll feel really good after you have cleaned up."

- Implement some creative ways to make it more enjoyable—or at least minimize the pain. "When life gives you lemons, make lemonade." Here are some ways to start squeezing the citrus:

  1. CONTEST: Pit sibling against sibling (rivalry will eclipse the toil).
  2. MAGIC: Twitch and blink like Samantha, Jeannie, and Mary Poppins.
  3. BOMBS AWAY: (Two-story houses only.) Dirty clothes over the rail into the hamper.
  4. SURPRISE: Place a treat under a mess. It's theirs after the mess is cleaned up.
  5. PENNIES: Give a penny for each item put away. (Well, just guess!)
  6. BASKETBALL: Deposit blocks in their container by way of jump and hook shots.
  7. ASSEMBLY LINE: Move the mess along a family chain to its final berth.
  8. MUSIC: Up the volume on the stereo with energetic tunes.
  9. CHALLENGE: Time the effort. Be done quickly for more playtime.
  10. PHOTOGRAPH: Take one of their immaculate room, and refer to it often.

Come to think of it, I did come close to never cleaning up—once. It was for two weeks in college, and it wasn't a pretty sight.

7. Trimming the Bushes   *"Mother Nature's Intentions"*

In moving through life, it is often not the result that is important but what was gained traveling down its road. It will help to remember this philosophy when you look at your once shapely bushes—the ones that never looked quite like the fancy ones in front of expensive homes, but look even less like them now—that your children just finished trimming.

"This could never occur at my house," you say, "because I would not let my children in the vicinity of bushes with clippers in their hands." Too bad, because there are many benefits to be achieved traveling down this road.

1. The children get to be just like Daddy and use real "Daddy tools." (Obviously, with real clippers, you need to provide real supervision.)
2. They can be creative with something more interesting than a paper hat.
3. They can affect nature (a big deal for a small child). You praise them for what they do—no matter what they do.
4. As they clean up—sweeping, raking, and disposing—they develop muscles, coordination, and the habit of finishing a job they start.

Yes, I hear you. "OK, my children made some strides here, but what about the state of my bushes? Should I have LET THEM do this? Will THE NEIGHBORS complain because they have to look at them? Should I go RE–TRIM them to see if I can salvage anything? Will PEOPLE THINK I can't do simple landscaping?" Don't worry about you, worry about your attitude and answer yourself this way:

*   LET THEM? Mother Nature intended for children to trim and clean up. Why else would she have given vegetation the wherewithal to grow back, and the trimmings the ability to decompose and blow away with the wind?

*   THE NEIGHBORS? Tell them your gardener is the police chief's son who is trying to earn extra money for college, and you couldn't very well fire him, merely because a *neighbor* told you to.

*   RE-TRIM? Mother Nature probably intended for her products to affect us, not for us to affect them, thus becoming slaves to her creations.

*   PEOPLE THINK? What people will think of you versus what is best for your children? No comparison, right? Unfortunately, our reflex response often favors the former.

8. Bathing the Dog   *"Technically, It's Not Torture"*

Our golden retriever's loyalty is always manifested on her face, as if to say, "I will do anything to please you," until she hears the word, BATH, and her name, GRETL, in the same sentence. Then I swear her expression changes to one of pleading, as if to say to me, "I was your first born. I've been with you longer than the children. Please don't let this happen, I beg of you."

Since I don't technically view a bath as torture, I usually give her the thumbs down, and we head for the bathtub. I have to believe my children take great pleasure in this experience, because they get to be in charge; they get to discipline; they get to dish out to the dog what we dish out to them. It sounds something like this:

"Gretl, SIT, or you will go to time-out."

"You're not behaving, and I DON'T LIKE IT."

"No, Gretl, no! You know better."

I laugh to myself thinking, *Gee, I hope I don't sound like that.* I'm sure it's a good catharsis for them, and I'm hopeful the power doesn't go to their heads. The dog survives with most of her dignity intact, and I generally make it up to her later with ball throwing or tasty table scraps.

The entertainment value is priceless. There is something precious about the innocence of dogs and children brought together with parallel purpose. My warped curiosity has often tempted me not to intervene at all and accept the consequences of cleanup afterwards, but wisdom has prevailed over nerve, so far.

Beyond the obvious benefits of joy and companionship that children gain from their pet, they reap the additional bonus of learning "hands on" about responsibility and the importance of respecting and appreciating living creatures. To disallow a pet in your household is to deny your children, and you, an important component of life's experience.

2

ADULT WORLD

- *Vacuum Cleaners*
- *Watches and Calculators*
- *Flying Down the Road*
- *Our Books and Magazines*

- *Spare Change*
- *Desk Drawers*
- *Home Improvement Stores*
- *Locks and Keys*

- *Supermarkets*
- *Kitchen Utensils*
- *Telephones*
- *Exploring in the Car*

Combine children's intense curiosity with their hunger to emulate us, and it's only a matter of time before they are investigating, examining, and manipulating many of the objects that populate our adult world.

This desire is further perpetuated, because Junior can't find a toy he wants to play with. Or when he does find the toy, it doesn't work. Or when he does find a toy, and it does work, it is often missing a piece. Or when he does find a toy, and it does work, and it isn't missing any pieces, he finds that the novelty wears off quickly. Or . . . *"Enough already!"* It finally occurs to Junior at some subconscious level that if toys were so much fun to play with, why don't Mom and Dad ever play with them?

Nowhere have I seen in the Rulebook of Life, a rule that states: "Children will not benefit or derive pleasure from anything other than toys or games targeted at them, and certainly not objects, places, and circumstances associated entirely with the adult world." Thank God, because with your ideas, guidance, and participation, a world that is generally mundane and second nature to us adults, is a novelty treasure chest of fun, games, and learning, to our kids.

. . . Like a Mister Potato Head or Barbie Doll.

9. Vacuum Cleaners   *"Mister Potato Head"*

I was never quite sure whether the word "vacuum" in vacuum cleaner was referring to the air properties of suction occurring as a result of the motor action, or the aftermath of running the vacuum when the carpet is a space entirely devoid of matter—or clean. Maybe it's neither. I suppose any word that has two consecutive "U's" in it can't be trusted anyway. Besides, when Mr. Spangler invented the first electric vacuum cleaner in 1908, it's an even chance he was attempting to invent the blow dryer, but got the wires crossed. With its dubious background, only one conclusion can be reached: The vacuum cleaner must be intended for children.

It whirrs like a toy airplane, has a light in the front like a toy choo-choo train, and has four small wheels like a toy car. Take off the hose from the canister, and you have a telescope or telephone. It has a variety of attachments for different configurations, so children can take them apart and put them together again like a Mister Potato Head or Barbie Doll. It has a cord that can be pulled all the way out and a button that can retract it all the way in. It can make things disappear off the carpet or out of thin air like magic. Some models are even child-sized, like a mini-vac. Although the advertising says mini-vacs are for large people with small messes, don't let it fool you. They really are for small people with *large* messes. And what toy is as indestructible as a vacuum cleaner? Nevertheless, like any children's toy, it's important to follow some simple DO's and DON'Ts when they use the vacuum cleaner.

DO let them suck toilet paper pieces out of the air before they hit the ground.
DON'T let them suck the entire roll of toilet paper off the roller.

DO let them vacuum the dog's tail.
DON'T let them vacuum the hamster's tail.

DO let them clean the dusty books.
DON'T let them clean the stamp collection album books.

DO let them extract the grime from the carpet.
DON'T let them extract grime from a diaper.

Here are some additional hints for you to follow: DO check the vacuum cleaner bag when you empty its contents, lest you spend a lifetime wondering whatever happened to Mom's ruby ring. DON'T fight with the children when you tire of the incessant drone and want the vacuum cleaner off; just throw the circuit breaker and pretend ignorance.

10. Spare Change   *"One Dollar Increments"*

If you have children, get comfortable with the reality that everything you buy will cost you in increments of one dollar. What this means is your spare change will no longer be available for you to use again. It will start out as "spare change," which you still can utilize for buying power, but it will move quickly to "used change," followed by "loose change," and ending up as "lost change." Let me elaborate. Spare change ceases to be spare, when it leaves your pocket or purse. It then generally moves into the used change phase, where children benefit from it, for learning and play. For example:

Change can teach:

- Basic counting
- Basic magic
- The great men on its faces
- The value of money
- The hobby of coin collecting

Change can be used for competitions by:

- Spinning it like a top
- Flipping it closest to the wall
- Rolling it for long distances
- Stacking it as high as possible

Change can also be used for:

- Rewarding good behavior
- Playing "heads or tails"
- Starting the custom of an allowance

The loose change stage means that it has, well, gotten loose. It is no longer available to teach and entertain. Generally you will find coins strewn all over the house, in out-of-way places, like rat droppings. When I do, I have a chance to take the change back into the spare change stage, but I usually can't, because I have on sweat pants that have no pockets, or my children are with me and they yell out, "My pennies! My pennies!" which moves the coins back into the used change stage. Often, I'm just too lazy to bend over for a few cents that I had already kissed good-bye, anyway.

The last stage, lost change, inevitably ends up as such, just like death and taxes, unless you are very ambitious and imaginative, in which case you can virtually take apart the house and reclaim most of it as spare change again. Nevertheless, is it worth it? I don't know, let's see:

2 children . . . 2 years apart . . . living at home = 20 years.
Mom or Dad finding $.37 cents in change every other day = $67.53 per year.

Hmmm . . . $67.53 a year! I think I will coin a new stage: The "romantic dinner for two" stage. Now, if you will pardon me, I have a date to take the house apart—and then one with my wife.

11. Supermarkets *"The First Disneyland"*

Contrary to popular belief, Mr. Disney did not conceive and construct the first mammoth family amusement park in 1955. Michael Kullen did, in 1930 twenty-five years previously, calling it a supermarket. (He must have felt the name Kullenland was too egocentric.) Yes, this is the very same place we mechanically wander through, often in a zombie state and generally alone, attired in sweats and curlers, or a five o'clock shadow.

We are doing it ALL WRONG!

The supermarket was designed as a family adventure, to be conducted on Saturday mornings, after showers and breakfast. So grab your spouse, seat belt your children into their roller-coaster shopping carts, and away you gooooo!

Accelerate down aisle one. Open the frozen-food doors. Get a frigid blast of air—burrrrrrr! → *Reach out and grab that instant coupon—missed. OK, here comes another one. Got it!* → *Smell that bakery aroma, ahhhhh. Watch that sharp turn! Whoa, made it.* → *Look. Free samples of pizza; take two. One for now, one for later.* → *There's a coffee grinder. Stop. WRRRRRRRRR. On to the next aisle.* → *Caution: Lobsters ready to charge at one o'clock! It's OK, kids, they're behind glass.* → *Toothless person at three o'clock; high sugar diet, kids.* → *Listen to that soothing music.* → *What time is it? No clocks here, in this timeless world.* → *Oh, oh. Here comes the scary part; sugared cereals at child-grabbing level. Hurry through. Whew! We made it.* → *Eeeee! Tropical water spray in the vegetable aisle. Take cover.* → *Alert, fit lady in the health-food section. Take note, kids.* → *It's "interaction time," children. Pick out a toothbrush and toothpaste. Good. You'll be more eager to brush, now. Throw those crackers into the cart. Pick out animal treats for the dog.* → *Time for reading practice. What's next on the list: A-P-P-L-E. Good! Next: J-E-L-L-Y. Good!* → *I think we're done! Look for a short line. There. No. There. No. There. Yes!* → *Watch out, impulse items! Candy, gum, toys, tabloid papers! Wow, close call.* → *OK, let's get the groceries on to the conveyer belt. Pile them on there and ring them up.* → *BEEP. BEEP. BUZZZZ. Try again. BEEP. Good!* → *Receipt, please . . . Ouch!*

Maybe we'll do Disneyland next week—I believe it might cost less.

12. Watches and Calculators   *"A Perfect Marriage"*

I recently let my youngsters play with two of my electronic devices: one that has an internal part that vibrates over 32,000 times a second, and one that can accomplish more than 400,000 calculations a second. Should I have my head examined for letting my children play with such sophisticated and expensive hardware? Hardly, since what I gave them to play with were calculators and watches that cost about as much as a good toothbrush; still functioning devices that had been superseded by even less expensive, more sophisticated models.

In the darkness of your drawers, you probably have enough discarded electronic calculators and quartz watches to fill a small shopping cart. Out there you have your children, who love your things—especially when they can hold them in their hands, push their buttons, and see immediate results.

You have the supply. They create the demand. We have a marriage. And what fruit will this marriage bear? With a calculator your children can:

1. Initially push the buttons and watch the display change while they sit on the potty, or ride in the car.
2. Gradually learn to count, as a numbers recognition induces a desire to learn.
3. Eventually learn the function keys as an introduction to basic math. They can work the calculator right alongside you, while you get your work done.
4. Probably save you the cost of a new stereo receiver. If they are going to play with a push–button electronic device, wouldn't you prefer they break a used $4.50 calculator instead?

What time is it? If we don't hurry we won't be on time. It's time for work, time for school, time to eat, time for bed. Time. Time. Time. Time. It must seem mysterious to children that a relatively artificial element controls much of what we do. Give them a watch, so they can start connecting with this "force." It will take awhile before they grasp the concept, but in the meantime, they will become engrossed in the display of numbers that have such power over you.

If the entertainment value of watches and calculators isn't enough, the money you will save in toy batteries, is enough to put your children through college. Heck, you might just as well give them every last calculator and watch you own. After all, while the children are enjoying the pleasure of those devices—those devices are making life difficult for you, reminding you that you are late, and over the family budget.

13. Desk Drawers   *"Parallel Worlds"*

Would you like to be able to do paperwork at your desk—paying bills, writing letters, updating household budgets, and so on—without constant interruptions and distractions from your toddlers? Of course you would, and you can! Pick the most likely solution from the following options and you are on your way.

A. Sedate Them   C. Terrorize Them
B. Bind and Gag Them   D. Give a Drawer to Them

Although all four would probably work, A, B, and C are probably counter-productive and quite possibly illegal. Therefore, why don't you give D a try?

Clean out the bottom drawer in your desk (oh come on, you have the room; you just need to re-organize a little), and tell your children it will be *their* very own drawer. Next, go on a scavenger hunt with your children to locate items that will be placed in their drawer. These items should be age-appropriate, favorite possessions, simple, easy to use, non-messy, and require little supervision. Here are some candidates:

Paper ✦ Pencils ✦ Doll ✦ Toy Cars ✦ Eraser ✦ Watch ✦ Calculator ✦ Ruler ✦
Necklace ✦ Crayons ✦ Coloring Book ✦ Scotch Tape ✦ Photographs ✦ Ball ✦
Kazoo ✦ Safety Scissors ✦ Paste ✦ Keys ✦ Toy Soldiers ✦ Flashlight ✦ Candy ✦
Kaleidoscope ✦ Hand Stamps ✦ Stickers ✦ Paper Clips ✦ Hair Clips

Now when you sit down to work, they can sit down "to work" alongside you. You say to them, "You have your work to do, and I have my work to do. You don't go in my drawers, and I don't go in your drawers." Not only will you get your work done, but your children will:

1. Feel grown up getting their work done.
2. Learn to put things away so they can be found next time.
3. Learn respect for your possessions (the items in the other desk drawers).
4. Take pride in their personal belongings.

Nevertheless, sometimes the best solution to solving a problem can have a downside. In this case I no longer have access to the kaleidoscope in *their* drawer.

14. Kitchen Utensils   *"Toy Room II"*

At the center of your child's universe is Mom, and quite often the center of Mom's universe is the kitchen. Logically then, your child will probably spend a great deal of time in that room of the house. Ho-hum, boring, right? Wrong.

The kitchen, in fact, could be the most exciting room in the house for your toddler. It is, after all, the very nerve center of your dwelling. Feeding into this room are gas, water, electrical, and communication lines. Terminated at the end of these lines are a whole array of appliances furnishing sights and sounds, tastes and smells, to assault the senses.

Toaster ✦ Can Opener ✦ Stove ✦ Microwave ✦ Blender ✦ Oven ✦ Dishwasher ✦ Coffee Maker ✦ Refrigerator ✦ Garbage Disposal ✦ Stove ✦ Stove Fan ✦ Mixer ✦ Phone ✦ Ice Maker ✦ Radio ✦ Faucet

There is enough action to hold the fascination of your child for a good while. When things are quiet in the kitchen and interest wanes, there is one last sense that hasn't been addressed to recapture his or her attention—touch.

Take a baby lock off one of your kitchen cabinets, fill it with some of the following utensils, and your child's sense of touch won't be denied for long.

Pots ✦ Pans ✦ Cups ✦ Plastic Bowls ✦ Containers ✦ Salad Spinner ✦ Scale ✦ Egg Beater ✦ Wooden Spoons ✦ Spatulas ✦ Ladle ✦ Whisk ✦ Basting Brush ✦ Garlic Press ✦ Tongs ✦ Ice Cream Scoop ✦ Nut Cracker ✦ Baster ✦ Rolling Pin ✦ Hourglass ✦ Oven Mitt ✦ Sponge ✦ Cookbook ✦ Coasters

Anything that isn't too sharp, too small, or too expensive. Then with those items he or she can:

Bang—Roll—Fit—Hide—Brush—Pickup—Squeeze—Stack—Spin—Turn—Wear

Later, when your spouse comes home and asks, "What are you making for dinner?" Your reply can be: "Reservations, Dear. How can I cook when the toy room is such a mess?"

15. Flying Down the Road   *"Where Are My Peanuts?"*

"He hit me! Stay on your side! Stop making faces! He's teasing me! He took my . . . "

"EXCUSE ME! This is your Captain speaking. You have just boarded PDQ Airlines, flight 1234, non-stop service to the corner market. We will be departing shortly, and flying at an altitude of 23,000 feet, at a speed of 600 miles an hour. Our in-flight movie will be *The Simpsons Meet the Flinstones*. Please sit back and enjoy the flight. And oh by the way, failure to comply with the 'No Fighting and Teasing' sign could result in the pilot's wish to fly this airplane into the ground."

Let's face it, it's a great solution in an environment of few options, when you're traveling in the car with the young ones. You can't send them to their room. You can't talk to them face to face. You can't blow up, lose your cool, and risk personal injury; or worse, knock over your commuter mug of coffee into your lap. You have squelched a squabble, and begun a game that will test their imaginations and challenge their creativity—and keep them from grabbing each other's throats.

Your children can be the copilots: "We're flying high up. We're flying fast. Put on your seat belt. Where's the landing gear?" They can be the flight attendants: "Here are the peanuts. Here is some water. Here is the blanket—go to sleep." They can be the passengers: "Where are we? Are we there yet? Where are my peanuts?" (Well, it's not so much what they say, it's the fact they are civil and quite possibly imaginative.)

To get you started on the road—I mean the air—here are 11 terms from the, Airplane-Automobile dictionary, to help bring realism to your excursion.

1. Pushing away from the gate (leaving the garage).
2. Taxiing to the runway (going down the street).
3. Taking-off (accelerating onto the expressway).
4. Ascending (going up the hill).
5. Banking (turning left or right).
6. Turbulence (hitting a pothole).
7. Autopilot (cruise control).
8. Circling (at a stoplight).
9. Flaps down (sun-visor down).
10. Landing (decelerating off the expressway).
11. Arriving at the gate (pulling into a parking spot).

Sure, I know. What do you do when your children are acting up on an *airplane*? Well, that's easy. Order a drink, ask for some peanuts, and put on your headphones.

16. Home Improvement Stores   *"Not Un-American"*

To enjoy and appreciate this activity, you must overcome our culture's belief that if you are doing something that isn't productive or goal oriented, then you are just wasting your time. So when I suggest there are times to stop and smell the roses, and that this is one of those times, I hope you won't consider me un-American. Take your children to the nearest home-improvement, or do–it–yourself store—not with the intention to buy, but simply to absorb and prod its surroundings. (I know it's painful, but try.) Observe and discover the 40,000 products, stacked to the top of the 30 foot ceilings in the one acre building, from air compressors to zappers (bug), and everything in between. You will come upon:

Lumber ✦ Plumbing ✦ Garden Supplies ✦ Electrical Equipment ✦ Flooring ✦ Paneling ✦ Tools ✦ Lights ✦ Riding Lawn Mowers ✦ Paint ✦ Doors ✦ Phones ✦ Kitchens ✦ Baths ✦ Cement ✦ Locks ✦ Hardware ✦ Fireplaces

Stroll up and down the wide aisles and watch:

- Fork Lifts at Work
- Lumber Being Sawed
- Keys Being Made
- Product Demonstrations
- Paint Cans Shaking in Mechanical Mixers
- How-To Videos

The atmosphere is festive and upbeat. The employees help you locate your items and pass along their knowledge. Consumers prepare to take on projects of building, repairing, and maintenance to save money and derive personal accomplishment. Unlike toy, candy, pet, department, and grocery stores, where things break, nutrition suffers, wallets thin out, common sense vanishes, and battles to buy are inevitable, in home improvement stores your children have virtually no temptation. Let them touch and guess what a particular item is or does. Teach and show them how things work. Allow them to wander and ask questions. It is one huge palace of three-dimensional free association.

As you leave the store, it may dawn on you that maybe, just maybe, you did accomplish something and the activity wasn't just a waste of time. Because if you left *that* particular store without a single purchase, that indeed would have been quite an accomplishment.

17. Telephones   *"Umbilical Cords"*

They are reproducing faster than rabbits. There are more than 500 million in the world, now. They began gradually, with one usually "tied-up" in the kitchen. Soon they were attached all over the house: master bedroom, living room, kitchen, and even bathrooms! Then they broke loose and became portable, roaming the house freely. Now they have found their way into automobiles, shirt pockets, and purses.

What is it about the telephone that requires us to have so many and to keep them so near at hand? Could the telephone represent the umbilical cord, regression back to a time that made us feel secure and connected? Possibly. Could it be that children's fascination with the phone might also be symbolic of the umbilical cord, but in their case represents *breaking* theirs, as the phone allows them expansion and the freedom to venture outside their confined world? Possibly. (Push a few buttons; hear a disembodied voice—a large body in the little phone?) Or could it be the author has read too much Freud? Probably.

Be that as it may, you will find your children more involved with the phone than a telemarketer is. So you might as well join them—because you can't beat them—and encourage some constructive and entertaining activities to channel their inquisitive energies. Here are 10 that work well:

1. Learning manners: Teach proper phone etiquette.
2. Taking messages: They can practice their letters and numbers (John: 555–1234).
3. Handling Emergencies: Learn 911, your address, and telephone number.
4. Playing with walkie-talkies: 2 phones + 2 children = 2 magpies.
5. Pleasing relatives: Call often to warm the hearts of Grandma and Grandpa.
6. Playing make believe (unconnected phone): For pretend conversations.
7. Learning about the insides (spare phone): Bells, wires, speaker (take apart and reassemble).
8. Maintaining friendships: Talk to friends (might save you a rainy-day drive to their house).
9. Talking on the "car" phone (spare phone): Long trips will seem shorter when they're occupied.
10. Talking on the presidential phone (unconnected phone): They can run the country.

TIP: Has your portable phone "roamed" out-of-sight with possibly some help from your children? Then pick up one of your connected phones, call a friend, and have he or she call *you*. Then just follow the ringing to your maverick phone.

18. Our Books and Magazines   *"Enough of Cruella"*

If your house is anything like our house, you probably have enough children's books to open up a small library. Strangely, you probably don't recall buying most of the books, do you? I'm not saying that these books don't have a lot to offer, because they do. Nevertheless, after the cat, of *The Cat In The Hat*, messes up Sally's house, for the fortieth time, or Cruella De Vil threatens, "Anita darling, what could you possibly do with all those puppies?" for the *101st* time, then it's time to consider some alternatives, for your sanity as well as your children's.

Have you ever considered reading to your children the adult material lying around your house? (No, not that kind.) Computer magazines, mail-order catalogs, travel books, how-to books, garden books, health books, *Sports Illustrated, Popular Science, Consumer Reports, Good Housekeeping*, and so on. Just about any reading material that contains pictures will do fine. Think about it. What is your goal when you read to your children? Most likely it is to build vocabulary, expand imaginations, and bond. Do the previously mentioned materials do this? Yes, they do, and in some ways better than children's books.

Which category of reading material often has a scary antagonist and ingredients for nightmares? Which category introduces your children to the real world and current events? You might say the adult material isn't a story, so it is more difficult to gain their attention and hold their interest. My children, however, don't follow along with children's stories much of the time anyway, and when that occurs, I improvise. Do the same with adult material. True, you have to work a little harder at it, but at the same time, you don't have to deal with Cruella, day in and day out.

Additionally, in case you haven't noticed, children are interested in what *you* are interested in. Your enthusiasm for your favorite material will usually generate the same energy in them. I'm not suggesting that you deep-six your children's books, just put them on ice for a while.

19. Locks and Keys   *"Anticipation and Exhilaration"*

If the lock and key had never been invented, it would be an indication we were living in a perfect utopia (or were always looking for our valuables). We have locks, it seems, for just about everything: doors, gates, suitcases, desks, boxes, bike chains, garages, cabinets, briefcases, cars, safes, tool chests, closets, and so on. I still remember the combination to my first bicycle lock (32–6–0). I was eight years old. My first recollection of a game show on television was a show called *Seven Keys*. On the show, a contestant won a new car if he or she selected the one key out of seven that started the car. The anticipation was excruciating; the turn of the correct key exhilarating. I was just seven years old.

No doubt you have a fond memory involving a lock or key. Maybe you currently have a prized possession under lock and key. Possibly you just get a good feeling when you turn a key, pull up, and hear the click of the lock. (Yes, maybe I'm carrying this a little too far, but you get the idea.)

Give your child a lock and key—preferably a matching set—and you probably will be surprised at the amount of time he or she will spend with it; opening and closing it, locking things up, playing make-believe. Next, if you have two children, initiate a contest between them. Who can open a lock first? Who can pick the right key, from many, that opens a lock? Who can pick the right key to open a cabinet that contains a surprise or a treat? Use this opportunity to explain about cherishing and protecting their own property, respecting other's property, and stealing.

Give your children a box, lock and key, and have them pick their most precious item to safeguard. The items they select often are insightful. (My youngest child picked a toothbrush, evidently after I explained about cavities and drilling). Additionally, using a lock and key improves your child's dexterity and hand strength.

Of course, someday when they win the car by picking the right key on the *new* present day *Seven Keys* show, your children will give it to you in appreciation of your having introduced them to this unique activity. (Uh Huh.)

20. Exploring in the Car   *"Aircraft Cockpit"*

You, Mr. Smithers, are sitting in the back of the coach section, quietly awaiting takeoff on a 747 jumbo jet, when a stewardess motions you to your feet. She takes your arm and escorts you up to the cockpit. Over the P.A. system, you hear the captain, "Flight 467, non-stop service to Chicago, will be delayed for a couple hours, while we allow Mr. Smithers to explore and play in the cockpit." Imagine the fun you would have pushing, pulling, and flipping every toggle, button, and control in the airplanes nerve center, working the flaps, rudders, engines, radar, and the other thousand or so controls at your reach.

Even though you will probably never have that opportunity—unless you own a major airline or have a verrrry long snow delay on the runway—you can give such an experience to your children. Because with everything being relative, the front seats of your car to your children, are probably the equivalent of the aircraft cockpit to you. So pull up a chair—I mean seat—actually the backseat, and invite your children to get into the front passenger compartment, and allow them "to explore and play in the cockpit."

It occurs to you while your children manipulate all that is within their reach, that car makers probably use children for testing to ensure their products can withstand the rigors of use. What will children do?

- THEY WILL: Honk the horn, turn on the headlights, lock the doors, open the windows, flip the visors, and turn on the radio.

- THEY WILL: Fasten the seat belts, play tapes, open the glove compartment, turn on the wipers, squirt the water, and turn on the interior lights.

- THEY WILL: Open the sunroof, move the seats, change the gears, push in the lighter (careful with this one), open the ashtrays, and release the emergency brake (it's all right, you're in the garage).

- THEY WILL: Adjust the mirrors, run the fan, flip on the blinkers, open the trunk, and push the trip odometer.

Of course, each of these acts must occur over and over again. By now, Mom, who is in the house will think Christine (the car from the Stephen King book and movie of the same name), has parked in the garage.

After a time, the children's imaginations take over and they play: firefighter, police officer, EMT (emergency medical technician), Daddy going to work, Mommy going to work, and of course, pizza deliverer. The experience, however, wouldn't be complete, if you didn't let them sit on your lap and assist in driving the car in and out of the garage. Just remember, though, the scene from the movie *Airplane,* and be careful as you pull forward.

3

IMAGINATION

- Clouds

- Playing Doctor

- Dress-Up

- Playhouses

- Shadows on the Wall

- Hand Puppets

- Playing Animals

- Spray Bottles

- Flashlights

- Stuffed Dolls

It's not intellectual, or is it logical. It's difficult to categorize or often understand. It's hard to qualify or even quantify. It's free form, unstructured, and frequently elusive. Because it's virtually impossible to measure, it is given little acceptance, or rarely cultivated, in the school setting. Parents denigrate it by making comments to their children such as, "You sure have a wild one," and "You need to stop day-dreaming." Furthermore, if all these negatives aren't enough, and you possess one that is *too* active, you may find yourself spending unwanted time at the Happy Acres funny farm.

The misunderstood trait is imagination; a trait that deserves a great deal more respect and acknowledgement than it's given.

Without imagination, many great inventions, discoveries, and contributions to mankind would never have come about. Only because great men and women thought beyond the bounds of conventional thinking and logic, structure, and academia, were advancements possible. Quite likely, imagination is even more evolved than intellect.

So what can you do to develop your child's imagination? Maybe nothing more than just letting it happen and not *discouraging* it. Seemingly, children start off with strong, inventive, and playful imaginations—an indication of the importance of imaginativeness—then somewhere between childhood and adulthood our fantasies get uprooted and die.

. . . Provides for a child the equivalent of ink blots.

21. Clouds   *"God Is Painting Again"*

"Look." I pointed up at the clouds in the sky. "God is painting again."

"How come God doesn't paint the clouds with colors?" my children asked.

"If God did, you couldn't see the rainbows as well, could you?" I concluded.

Oftentimes I have to answer their question with the question, "What do you think?" to avoid showing my ignorance. That time, however, I got away with an answer that just might be true.

Despite their seemingly boring black-and-white presentation, clouds can display a wide array of shades, shapes, and mystery that provides for a child the equivalent of ink blots, a sky of free association, and a trigger for imaginations.

Clouds can appear dirty, heavy, and threatening, or fleecy, cottony, and billowy. They can signal mist, drizzle, and sprinkles, or thunderstorms, hurricanes, and tornadoes. Will it rain or will it snow? Is that a mass, a bank, or a cover of clouds? Are those clouds, cirro, alto, or stratocumulus? (A comedy team of clouds?)

Clouds are the signature of the weather. They are used to describe contrasting moods of being on "cloud nine," or having a "cloud hang over your head." To a meteorologist, clouds are just cooling water vapor in the air, condensing into visible water droplets, however, to children they are a way to pass the time of day by scanning the skyline and blurting out,

"There's Barney the dinosaur."

"There's a pirate and a boat," my oldest detected.

"Look, Pamela Sue Anderson." (Well, I like to play too.)

"Santa Claus!"

"A duck!"

"A monster!" we proclaimed in rapid-fire order.

The clouds broke up and moved overhead. My youngest child cried because the pirate ship could no longer be found. I indicated it was still there, but a big cannon ball broke it into two pieces. My oldest child wanted to know whether they were the good pirates or bad pirates. I assured him they were bad. My children claimed to see a bee.

"Which cloud?" I inquired.

"There!" they pointed skyward.

Not seeing a cloud bee, I panicked, "Do you mean a cloud bee or a *real* bee?"

"Real! Real!" they shouted.

We decided this would be a good time to end the outdoor cloud game, and play an indoor—no danger of bees—game.

The next morning my oldest child woke up, looked out the window, saw no clouds, and began to cry. "I want to play the cloud game," he whimpered. "Where did the clouds go?"

I hesitated for a moment and then asked, "What do you think?"

22. Shadows on the Wall   *"Shady and Faceless"*

"Turn off the light switch and turn on the little lamp behind us. Now sit on the bed and I will tell you a story," I directed my children.

"This is a story about *shady* and *faceless* characters that follow us around, but who like to remain out of sight most of the time. You can find them at day or at night, inside or out. They enjoy boxing a few rounds, which is maybe why some people are scared of their own. On a sunny day, they might tell you the time, and one day a year, it's an even bet that the groundhog will see his own. Their favorite thing to do, however, is to masquerade as animals, and their favorite place to do this is on the walls.

"Now, I bet if you close your eyes, those pesky rascals just might visit this very room."

I held my hand up near the wall and manipulated my fingers until the shadow took the form of a rabbit.

"Look! Do you know what kind of animal this is? That's right, a chicken! (I figured it's more important to get them interested, than to defend my amateurish bunny.)

"How about this? Good, an alligator. Hold on, you can do it after I finish my story. What about this animal? It is a bird! Very good. Do you know which bird? Yes, it is Tweety bird! OK, you go ahead."

My children threw their hands in the air and wiggled their fingers. "Look, you just made an elephant!" I blurted out. "Can you do that again? Sure, I can show you. Here's how you do a rabbit. I'm sorry, you're right, it is a chicken. Look, I bet you can do this." I moved my arm in a wavy motion. "Right, a snake!"

"Ok. Let me finish the story. So there once was a rab . . . I mean chicken, alligator, Tweety bird, and a snake (I form each as I call them out), and their names were . . . Moe, Larry, Curly, and Shemp. Moe was their leader, so it was his responsibility to go to the pond every morning and get the breakfast bugs. On this particular morning, however . . . "

Just then Mom walked in the room and flipped on the light switch.

"Like I said, children, they prefer to remain out of sight most of the time."

23. Spray Bottles   *"Dorothy's Friend"*

Some people are born with the desire to play a musical instrument, others to play sports, and still a few others to learn a foreign language, but *all* of us are born with the hunger to propel water. The innate impulse probably dates back to either, the first caveman, Mr. Ogg, who tossed water on his first fire, or to Mrs. Ogg, who flung water on Mr. Ogg, for putting out a fire that wasn't seen again for twelve years.

Today the water-propulsion instinct can be channeled through one multipurpose device that provides hours of entertainment and make-believe, requiring virtually no supervision. If a child were as vulnerable to a fast-talking pitch man as an adult sometimes is, I can imagine he or she might see a TV commercial that goes something like this:

"Hey kids! Throw away your squirt guns, get rid of your pool toys, forget the garden hose, cast away your favorite water pail. Now YOU can be the first on your block to have the all-in-one, one-of-a-kind, kind-of-an-adventure, MULTIPURPOSE SPRAY BOTTLE. Spray, yes! But that's not all. It also streams, jets, mists, and squirts! Want to be a fireman? Set the dial to mist and cool down the coals in the fireplace before bedtime. Want to be a lawman? Set the dial to squirt and gun down the bad guys, or take target practice. Be a gardener and dial up stream to water the plants. Be a handyman and put it on jet to clean the windows and outside walls of your Mom and Dad's home. Dirty car in the driveway? Spruce up Mom's and Dad's tires and wheels in no time. But WAIT, there's more! Spray on yourself and your friends to keep cool in the summer. Fill with warm water and melt the snow in winter. Take to the pool for added water frolics. Take in the bathtub to spray the soap off your body. Move bugs along, clean your bike, and rinse the chocolate off your face. And when you're all worn out and thirsty from all this fun, fill it with your favorite beverage and squirt it into your mouth! And KIDS, if you act now, you will receive a 'Wicked Witch of the West' sticker. Just put it on your bottle, find her in Oz, and the sticker will entitle you to melt her away in ONE BIG SQUIRT— guaranteed."

24. Playing Doctor   *"It's Just Lipstick"*

It appears there are two kinds of people in the world: Those who don't go to the doctor until they absolutely have to, because of anxiety and phobias, and those who do go before the first postnasal drip hits the ground because of—anxiety and phobias. It's ironic that the subject we often know the least about, our bodies, is the subject we should know the most about. Maybe we can narrow the gap by influencing our children and future generations.

Because children visit the doctor regularly for checkups, colds, ear infections, *and* anxious parents, the doctor's visits are the perfect time to reduce the children's apprehension, increase awareness of their bodies, and provide some education. You can accomplish all this by incorporating the experience into their play. Take an old purse or a briefcase, and you have an old-fashioned doctor's bag you can fill with some of the following safe items for your children. Then, just let nature happen.

Band-Aids ✦ Vaseline (topical ointment) ✦ Penlight (ears, nose, and throat) ✦ Ice Pack ✦ Alcohol swabs ✦ Gauze ✦ Headphones (stethoscope) ✦ Athletic Tape Lipstick (blood) ✦ Food Colored Water (medicine) ✦ Meat Thermometer (shot) Calamine Lotion ✦ Dental Floss (sutures) ✦ Plastic Digital Thermometer ✦ Toy Camera (X-rays) ✦ Turkey Baster (nose or wound suction) ✦ Plastic Knife (scalpel)

If you have more than one child, they can take turns being the patient and the doctor, which allows you to observe and be thoroughly entertained at no cost. If you have one child, put on old clothes and prepare to be the vict . . . patient. You might want to have the video camera running, as the potential exists to capture moments worthy of submittal to the TV show, *America's Funniest Home Videos*.

Beyond the fun, education can take place while the children play. They will learn compassion and develop dexterity. You can enlighten them that doctors and nurses are their friends and are there to help, that medicine is not candy, and nutritious food will make their bodies work better. Practicing safety can reduce boo-boos. Additionally, you can take the opportunity to teach them about the parts of the body with pictures from a family medical book.

You might also want to mention in passing that doctors, can make a very good living.

25. Hand Puppets   *"Smelly Sock and Blankie"*

You have to wonder if children's imagination—the quality that allows them to believe a hand puppet is real—gets phased out over time due to the natural course of maturation, or if it is subtly suppressed by society's educational and socialization expectations. Maybe some of both. While this treasured capacity is still alive in your children, help provide the enjoyment that comes with it, by giving them a "hand."

Oh sure, you can turn on the TV and let hand puppets such as, Bert and Ernie, Kermit the Frog, or Lambchop entertain your children. Yet it's just not the same as having up-and-coming stars such as "Blankie in the Hand," and "Smelly Sock" come into your home in person. You say you're not familiar with these five-finger stars? Don't you read *Variety* or *Entertainment Weekly*? Well, I don't, either. I don't think you would find them in there, anyway, because these characters perform only in homes—and they can perform in your home, too.

If you can make a fist, find a flexible object to put your fist in, change your voice, and become *extremely* silly, you will have the pleasure of playing host to them, too. Blankie in the Hand came to life when my oldest child was three years old, courtesy of his baby blanket. Smelly Sock followed not too long after, and entertains both children with his many "faces and bouquets." When one of these characters mysteriously appears or is asked to do some spontaneous entertaining, the children come to life, not unlike as we might, when we see our favorite entertainer.

When we play this game, the children usually maneuver in close, eyes lit up and fixated on my hand, hanging on every word. Rarely do they look at me, except to request that I ask their puppet friend a question they are too shy to ask. Smelly Sock usually relies on physical humor, tickling, chomping off fingers, giving physicals as Dr. Sock, M.D. (Mildly Disturbed), and for attacking noses with intent to pollute. Blankie is more cerebral and manipulative, often using his celebrity status to influence good eating and hygiene habits. He often makes a point to herald the accolades of the children's parents.

Generally, you will tire long before your children do, and it becomes challenging to find a clever way to end the performance. Here's one approach:

"Ooooooo, stinky! Smelly sock, it's time to take a bath—into the washing machine with you. Blankie in the Hand—dirty, dirty, dirty! You follow right behind Mr. Sock." (The children throw the dirty birds in one after the other.) "Oh, Oh. Somebody else is stinky and dirty. Who could that be? It's time for the children to take a bath too."

There is nothing better than killing two birds with one stone—so to speak.

26. Flashlights   *"Sure, Dad"*

"Yes, it is true, son. The light *does* travel 186,000 miles a second. When I turn this flashlight on, the light goes so fast you can't even tell it's moving—really!" The blank stare I received from my child was probably appropriate. No doubt the concept was difficult for Carl Sagan to explain also.

No matter, because the flashlight has enough dimension and charm to hold the children's attention, anyway. Chances are you have half a dozen around your home and property; penlight to 6 volt, one battery to six, rechargeable or chargeable. Flashlights come in an endless number of varieties, but even greater are the number of games you can play with them. Here are 20 to get you started:

1. Play hide-and-go-seek at night, inside or outside.
2. Shine the beam of light at the sky and reflect it off the atmosphere.
3. Play *Star Trek* and beam people to you.
4. Use as a spotlight for a fashion show.
5. Hold two in each hand and be a car in a car race.
6. Hold one against your forehead and be a train.
7. Be one of 200 kids at camp with one and drive the staff crazy.
8. Observe the dust particles in the beam of light.
9. Play light tag or use it as a "death ray" in a game of war.
10. Direct people to their movie, sports, or concert seats.
11. Light it up under the blankets at night.
12. Hold under the chin and look frightening, then tell stories.
13. Play searchlights and open up an ice cream store or mall.
14. Look for birds and squirrels in the trees at night.
15. Hold on your palm and see the light through the back of your hand.
16. Play doctor or nurse and look in all the facial orifices.
17. Draw your name with light.
18. Play cowboy and see how quick on the draw you can be.
19. Give an SOS signal as a ship in distress.
20. Play cops and robbers (robbers case; cops search).

Then, for the next present giving occasion, what do you buy for your children? Well, of course— a large pack of batteries.

27. Dress-Up *"Off to England"*

Do you have a secret desire to travel to Buckingham Palace for the sole purpose of making the guards crack a smile, ruining tradition? If you're ever going to carry out this fantasy, may I suggest you get help from your children. It's quite simple. Put a pile of your clothes in a room with them, and wait an hour. When they are all "dressed up," get on the airplane and count the hours before you realize your fantasy.

My youngest child wearing my flannel shirt, Bermuda shorts, and dress shoes, appears like a child in one of those movies where some entity grants dad's wish to be a child again. With my tie around their necks, they tell me, "We have to go to work." My belt around their waists mystifies them, when it doesn't fit. Socks up to their thighs; shirts down to their knees. A pinstriped suit transforms them into midget gangsters. Say, "All right, you dirty rats," I prod. There has to be material for a sitcom in here, somewhere. When it occurs to me that one day these clothes will fit them, they'll be grown-up, and it won't be a game anymore, I smile a little less, and cherish them a little more.

They often pick clothes that express their natures. White T-shirts and black sweat pants for my sensitive and earnest child. Mickey Mouse boxer shorts and colorful socks for my impish and extroverted one.

Dress-up can even vent some unexpected expression of feelings. On one occasion my oldest child, showed real anger and exclaimed that, "I never have clean underwear!" When I asked him what he meant, he declared it upset him when I talked like that about Mommy not having the laundry done.

Through this make-believe game, I learned that my oldest wants to be a chef and work at a salad bar (which indicates a great desire to be highly specialized). My youngest wants to go to work and draw pictures. (Illustrators and cartoonist's can do well, can't they?) Laughter. Insights. Expressions. Goals. Whether you gain knowledge into your children's psyche or just have a good laugh or two, this pastime is priceless.

Oh, and don't forget to take your video camera on that trip to Buckingham Palace, otherwise no one will ever believe what you were able to accomplish.

28. Playing Animals   *"Join the Herd"*

It's a wonder that our children don't imprint to animals and become *them*, rather than us—human beings. Look at the content of the entertainment they are exposed to at a young age:

- Movies: (*101 Dalmatians, The Lion King, Dumbo*)
- Cartoon Characters: (Rocky and Bullwinkle, Bugs and Daffy, Yogi and Huckleberry)
- Puppets: (Bert and Ernie, Barney and Baby Bop, Bunny Rabbit and Mr. Moose)
- Books: (*Pooh Bear, The Cat in the Hat, Bambi*)

Oh, sure, there's Mr. Ranger, Elmer Fudd, Christopher Robin, Captain Kangaroo; no doubt, token "human beings" thrown in to keep us watching. So it's only a matter of time before you and your kids are on the floor imitating animals. You heard me right. *You* can't stay inconspicuous behind that newspaper for long before you are drawn in. Besides, here's a perfect opportunity to do two things: physically interact with your children, and be a child again. So, get on the floor, join the herd, and don't forget to take some "preposterous pills."

"Rrooaarr!" I grabbed my oldest child's leg and mauled him.

My youngest child jumped on my back. "Rrooaarr!"

"I'm an owl—whooo, whooo—follow me," I announced. We all tore around the house, arms flapping, "whooo! whooo! whooo!"

"Watch out," I said. "Sssssssssss. Snakes love to eat birds!" I picked up both my children and pretended to eat them.

"*Hee hee hee!*" they laughed hysterically.

"You sound like silly monkeys." We all laughed in unison.

"I'm hungry," spouted my youngest.

"Monkeys love apples," I announced. "Can you do this?" We lumbered and scratched our way to the kitchen. "Ee,Ee,Ee,Ee!!!" we screeched.

"Guess what animal I am," said my oldest. "Meow."

"A cat?" my youngest replied. "What am I? Woof! Woof!"

"Dogs chase cats!" I called out. "Go get the cat, I yelled to my oldest." They dashed on out the front door and around the front yard.

"Meow, Meow."

"Woof, Woof"

"Here I come." I lowered my head and placed my pointer fingers by my ears. "I'm a bull; watch out." I charged out the door, they screamed, and we ended up in a heap on the ground, wrestling like alligators. Recognizing that my respiration was three times greater than my kids, I decided to become a koala bear and then a turtle. Those ploys failed, however, so I became a shark, then ate them whole. Game over.

29. Stuffed Dolls   *"Always Check the Trash"*

Our plane is scheduled to leave in one hour for the family vacation. All of us are running hastily around the house in a panic, and it looks as if we are not going to make it. Which of the following is the most likely cause of this circumstance?

A. The airplane tickets can't be located   C. The car keys have disappeared
B. The travelers' checks can't be found   D. Tatters is missing

Misplacing A, B, or C, would be a minor annoyance compared to the life-shattering potential for the consequences of D. You see, Tatters, is my youngest child's inseparable companion, a simple, ragged, stuffed doll he goes nowhere without. NOWHERE. Why? Maybe because Tatters:

1. Provides more security at bedtime than searchlights and alarms.
2. Comforts my child in times of distress or loneliness.
3. Keeps my child's confidences safe and sound.
4. No longer makes my child the youngest child.
5. Is closer to my child's size.
6. Allows my child to yell at him up without retaliation.
7. Never says, "No," "Don't do that," or "Go to time-out."

And to ensure in the future that nothing threatens this relationship, I will keep the following list posted in plain sight:

1. Don't take it too far from home.
2. Always check the kitchen trash before dumping it.
3. Don't let anyone hang it out the car window.
4. Never attempt to wash it. (Corollary: keep it away from dirty diapers.)
5. Keep an eye on it when the dog is around.
6. Have two or three duplicates on hand, if possible.
7. Don't ever suggest to replace it with a look-a-like.
8. Keep tabs on it on a regular basis.

Yes, there are tradeoffs to having this inanimate friend for your child, but given the choice, I believe you should encourage it. More than likely your child's attraction and attachment to an inanimate friend will occur naturally; however, if it doesn't, here is what to do: Attend a garage sale and look for the, most tattered, pathetic, worn-out doll there, then grab it fast before someone else does.

30. Playhouses   *"Much Too Quiet"*

"Honey, do you hear anything?" my wife asked.

"No, what do you hear?" I said, baffled.

"I *don't* hear the children. They must be up to something."

An investigation revealed voices coming from under a card table draped with a blanket.

"What are you doing under there?" I inquired.

Giggles were the reply.

"It seems they are fine. They have a little playhouse." My wife looked pleasantly surprised.

It occurred to me that this was the first activity they had done together for any period of time not requiring our continuous supervision. What, then, made this particular endeavor so special? Having an area they could call their own and take pride in? Having privacy and sanctuary, perhaps time away from us, not unlike our requirement for time away from them? Having a small defined area scaled down to their size replacing the overwhelming world? I guess the "why" wasn't so important as the "what," and the "what," it appears, was "having a great time." My son came bounding into the kitchen, "We just played school and I was the teacher and I got to give homework!"

That week it was school. In weeks to follow they had a secret club where I think they paid homage to stuffed animals, a Mommy and Daddy sound-alike contest that involved a lot of scolding of make-believe kids, and a "getting dressed, drinking coffee, and having a hard day at work" discussion that sounded familiar.

Make-believe always kicks into high gear in this playhouse environment, although the locations change regularly (to stay a step ahead of inquiring parents, no doubt). Opening a closet to retrieve my coat one morning revealed an entrenchment on the floor—books, food, blanket, and toys. (Probably a lookout by which to spot suspicious parents.) Other popular domains include: guest bathroom, cardboard box, backyard wood shed, and the cavity under a desk.

"Honey, do you hear anything?" my wife queried.

"Nope. Pass the paper. I think we have a couple of hours to ourselves."

4

AEROBIC ACTIVITY

- *Dirt Piles*
- *Swimming Pools*
- *Playground Equipment*

- *In the Snow*
- *Cardboard Sleds*
- *Tag*

- *Wheelbarrows*
- *Sprinklers*
- *Leaf Piles*

Most people now recognize that aerobic activity is essential for maintaining a strong heart and healthy body, but few people would think of children as the target of this declaration. To encourage a child to be active may seem like having to tell a bee to make honey, or a bear to hibernate in the winter; children will just be active automatically. Might it be possible we are confusing physical activity with high energy?

In the electronic age pleasure and work is fed by coax cables, electric cords, and telephone lines. Computers, CD's, video games, faxes, the Internet, TV, radio, VCR's, and so on, serve only to exercise our eyes, and sometimes our fingers and minds. Maybe, then, it *is* necessary to be on the lookout for opportunities that will provide our children "huffing and puffing" time.

The benefits of physical activity are the same for children as they are for adults: Your children will feel better, look better, increase their self–esteem, make friends, sleep better, and increase their mental energy. Although the mind controls the body, the body also affects the mind. Additionally, the strong heart and healthy body they will require in adulthood will come much easier by way of good habits developed in childhood.

. . . Mt. Everest, Yankee Stadium, Disneyland, and the Moon.

31. Dirt Piles *"So Much for Progress"*

"Steep mountain! Steep mountain!" my children screamed as a home building site came into view, where an eight-foot-high pile of dirt awaited our assault.

A match made in heaven—children and dirt—and when a good amount of it is accumulated in one place, there is reason for excitement. I should clarify that to you and me it's a "dirt pile," but to a child, it's Mt. Everest, Yankee stadium, Disneyland, and the moon all rolled into one.

They studied the geography to determine the easiest route to the top. Then up they went, slipping, sliding, falling, and crying, negotiating the tough terrain with determination. Once at the top, it was time to take a breather, to reflect on the accomplishment, and to savor the view of the world below. Dirt clods became the object of the children's next activity, placing them on the mound, with two outs, ninth inning, seventh game of the World Series: Strike! Ball. Strike! Fast ball. Curve ball. Sinker ball. Multiple extra innings in this pitcher's duel. After the hard-fought game was over, it was time to relax, with a ride down the Matterhorn. *"Wheeeeeeeeeee!!!"* (Well, maybe relax wasn't the right word.) Careening down the mountain, they pushed the envelope at speeds too fast to measure. Nervous caution gave way to reckless abandon with each succeeding ride. As the perpetual motion machines began to lose momentum, the time came to dissect the monolithic giant and learn its secrets. The children dug, tunneled, picked, excavated, and burrowed until every rock, bug, paper, particle, and fragment were unearthed, examined, and reckoned with.

Fortunately, both the mountain and the children became exhausted at about the time daylight succumbed to darkness. As we headed home, a melancholy feeling set in with the realization that the steep mountain that was our friend that day would disappear with the erection of a new home within days. So much for progress.

32. In the Snow   *"Noah's Blunder"*

Noah Webster's *New Twentieth Century* dictionary defines snow as "particles of water vapor, which, when frozen in the upper air, fall to earth as soft, white, crystalline flakes."

Either Noah was king of the understatement or he was limited by his quota of words, because by leaving out what occurs *after* it has snowed he has done the word a great injustice. Maybe someday Mr. Webster's descendants will consider adding more information to the definition, so that you and your children will know all the possibilities, not unlike this:

Snow: A metaphor for a painter's blank easel that has no boundaries. A wonderland of free association and nature's endowment to humanity. As there are no two snowflakes alike, there are no two ways to experience a snowfall alike. If you feel:

- CREATIVE, you can: shape it, mold it, erect it, carve it, sculpt it, or transform it.
- ATHLETIC, you can: heave it, launch it, hurl it, toss it, or catch it.
- PRODUCTIVE, you can: dig it, shovel it, tunnel it, bank it, bucket it, burrow it, trench it, scrape it, disturb it, or remove it.
- DARING, you can: tumble down it, dive in it, glide on it, speed down it, sink in it, coast down it, skid across it, spin on it, jump into it, race down it, or maneuver through it.
- REFLECTIVE, you can: examine it, appreciate it, behold it, observe it, celebrate it, encounter it, anticipate it, hope for it, look for it, or survey it.
- EXPLORATIVE, you can: hike through it, stroll through it, shuffle through it, plod through it, wander through it, traipse through it, run through it, or crunch through it.
- ADOLESCENT (for the adults; kids can show you how), you can: melt it, compact it, stick it, squeeze it, eat it, or suck it.
- ARTISTIC, you can: draw it, sketch it, paint it, or photograph it.

And, if *you* ever get tired of doing things in it and want to take a break, send your children out to find two snowflakes that are alike. (Yes, that is cruel.)

33. Wheelbarrows   *"MPC — Miles Per Calorie"*

Which item below might be considered a child's version of an all–terrain vehicle that he or she can utilize as a roller coaster, material transporter, yard waste hauler, and child's maintenance trainer? A device that is simple, has few parts, and is virtually indestructible.

A. A Crystal Vase

B. The Space Shuttle

C. Grandma

D. A Wheelbarrow

If you chose A, B, or C, you clearly have a vivid imagination and for that you get partial credit; however, the versatile, enduring wheelbarrow, usually relied upon as a multi-purpose apparatus for adults can also be the focal point of a child's pleasure.

The colorful uni-wheeled chariot provides exciting, energy-efficient rides, running on "Daddypower," which gets infinite miles to the calorie (MPC). Through the grass, up the dirt incline, over the curb, onto the asphalt, across the front lawn, and down the gravel hill. With multiple surfaces and no track, each ride is a unique adventure as the wheelbarrow bounces up and down, left and right, at the mercy of the terrain. The efficient emergency braking system (two back pods) halts progress, and an automatic disembarking system (I dump the children out) places them gently in the grass. Loading, transporting, and unloading numerous materials from the yard-shuttle, such as leaves, trash, sand, garden tools, bricks, sod, dirt, rocks, firewood, and fertilizer, comes in a close second to the fun of the trackless roller coaster ride.

After the rides and work are done, the children can get training in basic maintenance by helping to ready the wheelbarrow for its next assignment. They can hose it down, clean it up, pump up the tire, tighten the bolts, oil the axle, and maybe add a coat of paint.

No doubt one day *my* children will be pushing *their* children around the yard, in the very same wheelbarrow, as I look on sipping iced tea, getting misty eyed.

34. Swimming Pools   *"Links to the Past"*

Water might be one of the few pleasures in life that equally pleases the infants who are thrilled by it, the middle–aged who are invigorated by it, and the elderly who are calmed by it. Yet, it is completely passive, made up simply of two parts hydrogen and one part oxygen. This body of standing matter can be public or private, indoor or outdoor, heated or unheated, above-ground or in-ground, large or small, yours or a friend's.

The swimming pool is a link to the past, which may in part explain its universal attraction. We emerged from the primordial soup of the oceans, lived our first nine months in the warm waters of the womb, and are composed of approximately 90 percent water. A child, just having left the womb, probably feels more at home in a pool than he or she does on land.

Observe your children's expressions as they play in the water, and you'll probably agree. Watch them as they splash, kick, float, sit on a step, and dangle their feet; jump in, put their head under, blow bubbles, throw a ball, and dive under for an object; sit on your shoulders, and bounce up and down in your arms. Watch them as you teach them to swim, when you hold them horizontal, spin them around like a wild motorboat as you hold their hands, throw them up, and catch them. As additional testimony to the power of the swimming pool, I can say with my best recollection, that I have *never* seen a child:

1. At the pool with a sad face (until they are told it is time to leave).
2. Complain the water was too cold.
3. Sleep restlessly after a day in the pool.
4. Not be able to entertain himself or herself.
5. Fall asleep at the pool.
6. Misbehave when threatened with losing pool privileges.
7. Unable to make a friend at the pool.
8. Want to get out of the water.
9. Without a voracious appetite after an hour in the pool.
10. Turn down the opportunity to go to a pool.

And not give a bear hug to parents for taking them to the swimming pool.

35. Cardboard Sleds   *"In Our Fabric"*

The following quiz is designed to test your ability to think like a child. For which one of the following is your child most likely to want to use a cardboard box for?

    A. In a three-dimensional, stationary state holding old rags?
    B. In a flat two-dimensional, stationary state soaking up oil drips?
    C. In a three-dimensional, stationary state as a kitty litter box?
    D. In a flat two-dimensional, in-motion state as a downhill sled?

If you guessed A, B, or C, or had to think about it before you answered, or thought an *in-motion* state was California, then just give the box to your child and trust his or her instincts. It appears, built into the fabric of each and everyone one of us is the desire to GO FAST. No doubt, long ago, there were sound evolutionary reasons for this instinct (running after your food, or running to keep from becoming food). Today though, moving quickly is probably no longer necessary, yet the instinct remains.

    All I know is, when you give your child a flattened cardboard box, on any smooth surface with an incline, you can witness the instinct by the way of hearing and seeing first hand.

YOU WILL HEAR:

"It's my turn." ✦ "Let's all get on." ✦ "Wait for me!" ✦ "I want to sit in front." ✦ "Not yet, I'm not ready." ✦ "Ouchhh!" ✦ "Hold on!" ✦ "Faster, faster, faster." ✦ "Eeeee!" ✦ "Slooow dooown!!" ✦ "I'm falling off!" ✦ "My bottom hurts." ✦ "Let's do it again!" ✦ "Whoooooh!" ✦ "Aaaahhh!" ✦ "Go this way."

YOU WILL SEE:

Beaming faces ✦ Wide eyes ✦ Seated positions ✦ Crashing ✦ Standing positions ✦ Going backwards ✦ Going sideways ✦ Tumbling ✦ Children on their backs ✦ Going forwards ✦ Spinning ✦ Falling ✦ Kids on their stomachs ✦ White knuckles ✦ Mouths and bodies in perpetual motion.

When the cardboard sled is tattered and ragged, unable to negotiate one more incline, you'll be able to retire it to the garage floor, where it will live out its days absorbing oil drips. Where, then, will you get a *new* bobsled? Probably from the kitty litter or old rags box.

36. Sprinklers *"Lawn Growth, Too"*

You look out the window and your children are running out of control, arms flailing, screaming hysterically. You can bet they are reacting to:

      A. A nearby airplane disaster
      B. A swarm of killer bees
      C. A cluster of alien saucers approaching from the north
      D. A geyser of water shooting from the lawn sprinkler

If you see water spraying, then most likely you picked D. If you don't see any water, however, you should simultaneously panic and take some form of action.

Whoever invented the lawn sprinkler I'm sure did so, not to become more efficient in lawn watering, but to provide children an alternative to a swimming pool. It was only by accident, after observing the tremendous improvement in lawn growth, did the sprinkler became a lawn-maintenance apparatus.

On a sweltering day, the lawn sprinkler has triple appeal.

1. It's immediate gratification; three steps outside and a turn of a valve.
2. Unlike a pool or a bath, the water is in motion; agitated, pulsating, and spraying.
3. With sprinklers intended for something other than a child's toy, the attraction is that much more appealing.

Now it's time to play in the sprinklers, so let's:

1. Run full speed through them.
2. Look for the rainbow.
3. Jump through the stream and over the jet.
4. Swing and hit the water with a hand or paddle.
5. Catch the water in a cup and pour it over someone.
6. Launch a plastic ball in the jet stream.
7. Sit on the sprinkler head to suppress the flow.
8. Take off the sprinkler head and frolic in the geyser.
9. Outrun the spray as it changes direction.

While you watch the children in perpetual motion, you can't help wondering why Jane Fonda hasn't yet produced an adult aerobics video entitled, *Romping Through the Sprinklers With Jane.* Of course, with her leading the way in her water-slicked bathing suit, I'd buy it . . . for my wife.

37. Playground Equipment   *"Ancient Torture Device?"*

With the arrival of computers, video games, interactive TV, and electronic gadgets, playground equipment might long be forgotten and abandoned. Excavating archeologists, may one day come upon these apparatus, and scratch their heads in bewilderment.

"Hey Joe, over here. Look! An ancient torture device."

"No, Sam, I believe we have uncovered a city zoo."

We can only hope it will never come to this. Those sturdy steel structures of diversity can provide the predominant means for a young child to develop his or her muscles, strength, and coordination, when the window of opportunity is optimal. Additionally, the heart muscle gets a workout as well as social skills (a euphemism for: "I was here first! I don't wanna share!"). Here are some of the more common playground items and how they benefit various muscle groups:

1. Teeter-totter (calves and thighs)
2. Rings and monkey bars (arms, shoulders, back)
3. Swings (upper legs)
4. Merry-go-round and slide (arms, legs)
5. Tubes (neck, back)
6. Jungle gym (most muscles)

Although children tend to be pulled like a magnet to anything breakable, this play item won't be subject to that hazard. True, I guess the tradeoff here is that the *children* are the ones prone to breakage. Nevertheless, with your supervision, and some hands-on demonstration (no, you're never too old), the risk will be greatly reduced.

Playing at the playground may seem like an activity that will naturally occur, because you have active children, and playgrounds are everywhere. Ask yourself this, though. When was the last time your child had a good workout on the playground? When was the last time your child sat spellbound in front of the television?

38. Tag   *"The First Game"*

"You're it!" If someone comes running at you, touches you, says this, then runs the other way, there is probably a high degree of certainty you understand and know what to do. (If this occurs at work, however, stay cool and pretend nothing happened, unless it's your *boss*, in which case you may consider playing along and chasing after a fellow worker.)

Tag might just be *the* universal game. It may well have been the first game ever played. One caveman clubbed another over the head. He felt guilty and exclaimed, "Your hit." After which they took alternate blows. As humans became civilized, the clubbing became a gentle tag with the hand and the "Your hit" became "You're it."

With no boundaries, equipment, or rules per se, and a one-sentence explanation on how to play, tag has to be the quintessential game for children. A hand and some mobility are all that's required. On the front lawn, we all look like agitated atoms colliding frantically, chasing, and fleeing. I have to crawl, run backwards, and tag with my elbow to make it fair when I play with my children.

A cul-de-sac provides a great playing field. Sometimes a big beach ball is substituted for a hand as the "tagger." A living room offers the stage for a game of Marco Polo, where I have to seek and tag with my eyes closed. Laughter abounds as tripping and bumping eventually culminates in tagging the unsuspecting dog. The park playground becomes the next backdrop as a piece of adhesive paper is used as the tagger. Hysterical laughter and physical exhaustion eventually ends the game.

Tag enhances the children's stamina, speed, agility, and preparedness. Preparedness? Why yes, for the 2020 Olympic Games when tag will be the premiere sport. (Well you never know.)

"How is Olympic tag played?" you ask. Well, 1,000 competitors start on a soccer field and play until only one is left. Here are the rules:

Every entrant wears a vest that lights up when tagged. Tag unlighted competitors, and the vest turns yellow and they are "it." Tag competitors that have turned yellow, the vest turns red, and the competitors are eliminated, but you are still "it" until you tag an unlighted individual. If, after five minutes, you haven't tagged someone, you are out, and the person you are closest to at the time is "it."

Follow that? Don't worry. Just keep playing tag, and I'll get back to you in 2020.

39. Leaf Piles   *"The Missing Stage"*

Some things you learn in school, and some things you need to find out for yourself. Beginning science taught me that leaves produce oxygen as a byproduct of photosynthesis, then fall off the limb to help the trees survive the winter, and finally decompose to produce fertilizer to spur their growth.

PHOTOSYNTHESIS → OXYGEN → FERTILIZER → TREE GROWTH

Right? Wrong. Our textbooks suspiciously left out a stage, probably because it would lead to play and distract us from our schoolwork. Now that we are older, we all know it as the "leaf pile," or AMUSEMENT stage, which comes between the oxygen and the fertilizer stage.

PHOTOSYNTHESIS → OXYGEN → *AMUSEMENT* → FERTILIZER → TREE GROWTH

Mother Nature must have intentionally created the amusement stage by painting her leaves with many beautiful colors to attract the children, who in turn manufacture the pile. She added the breeze that blows in the fall to create a cushion between the thin leaves, for softer landings. The breeze later increases to a wind, to distribute the leaves prior to decomposition and fertilization. If this scenario seems a little hard to swallow, then watch kids playing in a leaf pile for a while, and you'll know what Mother Nature intended.

Just observe and note: "Ready, set, go." I announce. They rush full speed ahead, throw themselves head first into the heap, then burrow deep until they disappear. They come up tossing leaves every which way, then stop to appraise the situation. They crawl out of the pile and evaluate the effect of their intrusion. They perform some minimal raking maintenance and then go back at it.

I hide a ball in the middle. "Who can find it first? Ready, set, go!" Chaos reigns as arms and legs appear separated from bodies. "Move!" "I've got it!" "No!" "Ouch!" "Where is it?" The dog joins the fracas and retrieves the ball while barely disturbing a leaf.

Children chase dog. Dog leaps into pile. Children leap on dog and bury dog under leaves. Mom takes some photographs. Dad adds more leaves. Mother Nature smiles from ear to ear.

5

FAMILY ROOTS

- *Storage Rooms*

- *Fireplaces*

- *Parent's Old Neighborhood*

- *Photo Albums*

- *Wedding Albums*

- *Home Video Replays*

- *Visiting Grandparents*

Some say that the family unit is the "dirt from which everything grows," the "foundation from which everything is built," and the "diving board from which everything springs." Some would say these people need to burn their book of metaphors. Generally, though, almost everyone agrees that a child's chances for happiness, success, and even survival, are greatly improved when he or she grows up attached to some kind of nuclear unit, one where the child receives love, guidance, security, and acceptance.

Over time, your children will become cognizant of the entity called "family," and as they do, you will have the opportunity to reinforce the concept and amplify the meaning.

By introducing situations of family fortification like the ones presented in this chapter, you can influence the strengthening of family and reap all the benefits that go along with it. As the idea takes hold in the soul and spirit of your children, you will no doubt start to see the fruits of your investment: the eagerness in their walks, the confidence in their talks, and the serenity in their hearts.

. . . Unless you move or misplace your winning lottery ticket.

40. Storage Rooms   *"Expanding Time Capsules"*

If the adage, "A place for everything and everything in its place" is such a time-honored proverb, why do so many people have closets, garages, attics, basements, and spare bedrooms full of things essentially *not* in their places? Is it because we were given only one place to put our things, so that when we got a new thing, the old one had no place to go, except into one of the above-mentioned places, that apparently is *not* a place? (*Huh?*) Over the years, these areas of your home seem magically to accumulate your material possessions, and unless you move or misplace your winning lottery ticket, those spaces go undisturbed. Too bad, because those expanding time capsules have much to offer your children—and you. So take your children by the hand, lead them to the attic, and discover buried treasure. You can:

1. START A HOBBY after finding an old coin, doll, or baseball card.
2. REVERE FAMILY by unboxing your wedding dress and sharing feelings about love, marriage, and your children.
3. DISPLAY A SOFT SPOT IN YOUR ARMOR and show them the C minus you received in math on your fourth-grade report card, revealing math was hard for you, too.
4. LAUGH TOGETHER at the record player and reel-to-reel tape recorder, and explain to them about the good old days of the *uncompact* disc and annoying hiss.
5. FORTIFY YOUR CHILDREN'S HERITAGE with the dusty photograph of great-great-Grandma Gertrude who made thread with a spinning wheel and owned the first refrigerator in her neighborhood.
6. INTRODUCE YOUR CHILDREN TO NOSTALGIA (it's never too early) by displaying their baby bath and infant clothes.
7. ENCOURAGE ASPIRATIONS by honoring your cheerleading outfit and track uniform.

If, on some level, your children haven't gained something after taking a joy ride through your forgotten relics, then try these ideas:

8. Explain about less fortunate human beings, and have the children pick out items to give to CHARITY.
9. Have a garage sale whereby if they help and participate, they can keep the proceeds TO SAVE AND BE RESPONSIBLE for.

Then after donating items to charity and holding a garage sale, let the children take ownership of the new empty space, where they can organize and have—a place for everything and everything in its place.

41. Photo Albums   *"On the Fridge"*

Perfect! You have just arranged your holiday snapshots in the photo album—chronologically, neatly, and with maybe an appropriate description accompanying each photo. You're proud of the fact that you took the time to organize the pictures, so that they would be accessible and comprehensible, whenever the whim hit you to view them.

But life moves forward, and you're on to your next adventure, with more snapshots, and more organizing, and the cycle repeats itself. Before you know it, your kids are grown and gone. The album was never opened after its compilation, and you may not be able to find it now. If found, it's probably in a degenerative state, not unlike you, and your memory can't quite associate the photographs with the events that took place, paralyzing your walk down memory lane.

"Well, thanks," you say, "for making my day a little brighter. I hope there's a point to this motivational speech. What do you want me to do, get rid of my camera?"

I'm sorry, but my intentions are purely honorable. You should not get rid of your camera, but you *should* get rid of the notion that your photographs and albums are only for viewing at times when you are feeling nostalgic or melancholy. Instead, take them out every few months and enjoy them with your children. Here are 10 good reasons why:

1. ANTICIPATION: Browse photos of past events (Christmas, birthdays, 4th of July), just prior to their recurrence.
2. GAMES: Play guessing games such as: "Where was this taken? How old were you here?"
3. REMEMBERING: Help children recall relatives and friends that live far away.
4. THREE-DIMENSIONAL PARENTS: Amaze children with pictures of you and your spouse through the years for amusement and perspective.
5. SELF ESTEEM: Have your children pick out and carry around photos they are proud of.
6. ROLE MODELING: Show how Mom and Dad excelled in their youth (cheerleading, running track, riding a two-wheel bike).
7. AMUSEMENT: Present the children baby pictures of themselves.
8. FAMILY TIES: Strengthen family closeness with vacation, holiday, and event photos.
9. ICE BREAKERS: Show your children relevant photos of you, to ease their "first time" insecurities (school, swim lesson, dance).
10. REDIRECTION: Use photos to divert attention away from sibling squabbles.

Now, as a reminder for this activity, take a picture of your photograph album and place *it* on the refrigerator door.

42. Home Video Replays   *"Almost Oblivious"*

If photographs are a moment frozen in time, then what must videotapes be—a facsimile of time? What *we* would give to have hours upon hours of our early lives captured in trouble-free, compact videocassettes, like our children probably have. Then, within seconds of a whim, we could relive the experiences exactly as they happened, just by nudging a "little case" into a machine Every little detail, as it was then, as it will be forever. Life moves forward, except in these cassettes. It's no wonder why my children are oblivious to anything else going on around them, when they watch videotapes of themselves and the family.

"Kids, dinner," I called. (No response.)

"We're having chocolate cake." (No response.)

"Look, Barney the dinosaur just walked in. (No response.)

"Here's a gallon of paint; would you paint the inside of the house?"

"Yeah, Dad!!!" (Well, almost oblivious.)

Whoever said children have short attention spans and can't concentrate for any length of time didn't avail themselves of the home videos. Similar to the gains realized with photograph albums, here are even more benefits available by walking down video memory lane:

- CORRECT ORDER: They watch our wedding video, *then* see pregnancy footage of my wife. We hope they are influenced by this sequence.

- THE TALK: They love to see their mother's labor and their deliveries on tape. "The talk" I have with them someday should go a little smoother because of that.

- FEEDBACK: They see who and what they are. They see what they like and what they don't like about themselves. They build stronger egos and identities. Metaphorically, they see that they really are somebody.

- LOVE: They see themselves being cared for as babies (diapering, bathing, feeding, washing, and so on). On some level, this communicates that they have worth and are loved.

- BRAINWASHING: We say, "Look how *small* you were then and how *big* you are now! Must be all those vegetables you are eating."

- CANDIDATES: Have them identify those funny moments that would be perfect for *America's Funniest Home Videos*.

- CONTEST: Stick in a video tape and ask who can be the first to guess correctly the four W's. WHAT are they doing? WHERE are they? WHY are they doing it? WHEN did it occur?

You know, it's quite possible playing home videos might make the television a useful device after all.

43. Fireplaces   *"Warm Television"*

What object in your home hypnotizes you, puts you to sleep, invites make-believe, and brings the family together? Television would be a good answer, if it were not for the particular title of this piece. How about if I said it warms you; provides an entrance for Santa Claus; makes a tasty, gooey marshmallow; and "burns," but never catches fire. Yes, the fireplace! How smart you are. The following scene should help illustrate its value to children, and serve as a metaphor for family harmony.

The television fades into the background as the fireplace takes over the family's attention.

MOM: "Good fire, Honey."

DAD: "Thanks."

OLDEST: "I put the wood in!"

DAD: "Yes, you did."

YOUNGEST: "I wit it! I wit it!"

DAD: "Yes, with my help you lit the fire."

OLDEST: "Errrrrrrr!! Here comes the fire truck. Need to put up the ladder. I got the hose. Shooooo!! I'm putting out the fire. I'll save you! Can we do marshmallows, now?"

DAD: "No, we have to wait until the flames are reduced to coals."

YOUNGEST: "I'm cold."

MOM: "Come toward the fire, little one, and you'll warm up real quick."

DAD: "Not too close, though. You have to have great respect for fire. The same fire that can warm your house can also burn it down."

OLDEST: "We better not have a fire when Santa comes."

MOM: "Yeah, I don't think that would make Santa feel very welcome."

(One hour later)

DAD: "Do you realize how long our children have been transfixed by that fire?"

MOM: "Too bad we can't use it as a baby-sitter."

DAD: "Do you think I should put another log on?"

OLDEST: "No, Dad! You said we could toast marshmallows."

DAD: "Here, give me your coat hanger. There you go."

OLDEST: "Dad, do you like the fire smell?"

DAD: "Believe it or not, it's one of my favorite odors. It brings back memories of singing around the campfire at summer camp, roasting weenies at the beach, and being in the snowy mountains."

(One hour later)

MOM: "Did you notice that the flicker of the flame died out at about the same time as the children?"

DAD: "Yeah. Hey, you know what memory I forgot?" *Smoooch.* "The memory
of me romancing you by the fire."

MOM: "Ahhhhh." *Smooch, smooch.*

44. Wedding Albums   *"Funny-Dressed Man"*

If you think your wedding album's sole purpose is to be opened only on your anniversary, after consuming a few drinks, to have a good laugh over how efficient the aging process is, then think again. Because, buried in the pages of those two-dimensional 8 x 10 inch glossies is a three-dimensional, real life textbook, ready at anytime to introduce your offspring to some of our culture's most revered institutions: marriage, religion, friends, children, family, tradition, and social graces. So pull up a child and share these riches—and yourself.

Here was my side of the conversation, as I shared our wedding album with my four-year-old.

"Yeah, that *really is* Mommy and me. These pictures were taken the day we got married. Well, getting married is kind of like you wanting to hang out with a special friend, all the time, and no one else. Why? Well, it's kind of like Daddy being a battery, and Mommy being a battery operated toy; we work a lot better together than we do apart."

"That man dressed in a funny way is a minister. He is here on behalf of God to make sure Mommy and Daddy are right for each other, and he gives us permission to hang around together forever, no matter what happens."

"All these people are here because they're our friends. They make having fun in life, a lot more fun and they make being sad, a lot less sad."

"No, *you're not* in that big crowd of people. One reason we got married, however, was to prepare for you, and that very night we started practicing real hard."

"Many of those people are your family. They are related to you, and have all given a part of themselves to you. See, you kind of have Aunt Patty's eyes."

"No, Mommy is not *throwing away* the flowers. That's a tradition. Well, even though it seems silly, we do it because it is a way to make this day feel complete, like it all really happened, I guess."

"You're right, everyone does look pretty. It's a day when all the people are at their best. They look their best, act their best, have their best table manners, and are the most polite they can be."

"What? It all sounded great, until now?"

45. Visiting Grandparents   *"Deep Roots for Growth"*

Some of my earliest and fondest recollections were of some older people who held me on their laps, helped me drink from a cup, and patted me on the back. In addition, they looked down at me with a warm smile, showed interest in all I said, and never judged my words or raised their voices. I was told these special people were something called grandparents—and *grand* they were.

Failure to appreciate how much your children can benefit from time spent with their living heritage would be a mistake; a poignant loss to their lives that has no substitute. Here are 10 ways, out of perhaps hundreds, that the more *mature* family members can help the less mature ones:

1. MISTAKES: Alert the grandchildren to errors that they, the grandparents, have made.
2. APTITUDE: Recognize and encourage a hereditary talent.
3. OBJECTIVITY: Observe aspects of the grandchildren that the parents might be blind too.
4. YOUTH: Provide a presence so grandchildren can appreciate their own adolescence.
5. COMPASSION: (if disabled) Awaken the quality of kindness in their grandchildren.
6. BELONGING: Increase the feeling of grounding by widening the family foundation.
7. BALANCE: Be what parents sometimes cannot afford to be.
8. PACE: Display a relaxed manner and a sense of calm.
9. PERSONALIZATION: Share anecdotes about the grandchildren's parents to humanize them.
10. LOVE: Dispense a special kind of devotion that only a grandparent can provide.

Now that the years have gone by, and your children now have children, and Grandma and Grandpa are gone, it is my hope you hear the words from your children, "I wish I could be just like Grandpa," rather than, "What was Grandpa like?" Because if you hear the words, "What was Grandpa like?" you as a grandparent are likely to suffer the same consequences as Grandpa did. While you are sitting in your rocking chair wondering why your children and grandchildren never come around, remember back when you didn't take the time to bring your children and grandparents together, and you will have answered your own question.

46. Parent's Old Neighborhood   *"I Was a Child"*

The following conversation took place between my three-year-old and me:

ME: "I was too."
THREE-YEAR-OLD: "No you weren't."
ME: "I was *too* a child! Grandma is *my* Mommy."
THREE-YEAR-OLD: "No she's not."
ME: "Yes, she IS."
THREE-YEAR-OLD: "No, she's not."
ME: "And someday *you* will have children, and I will be *their* grandpa."
THREE-YEAR-OLD: "Noooo!"
ME: "Yeeees! OK, into the car, we are going for a little drive."

If young children could articulate their feelings, they would probably grumble that their parents were conceived as adults, with the purpose in life to order them around, tell them NO, and prevent them from having fun. I believe, however, that it is possible for parents to help bridge the child-parent gap—OK, chasm—by remembering what it was like to be in their children's shoes, and for them to realize that we once were. Here was my side of the conversation as we took a car ride back in time.

"There it is. That's where I went to elementary school. Over there on the playground is where I split my pants up the middle playing foursquare. I ran home in embarrassment. See that wall by the playground? I threw wet, colored, crepe paper at that wall and stained it. I got into BIG trouble over that."

"That's the house where Grandma raised me. I loved my front yard. I spent hours throwing a ball against that garage, pretending to be a big-league pitcher. Looks like they've painted it."

"See the street curb there in front of the house? I spent a whole afternoon floating leaves down the rain gutter and crying when my best friend didn't show up to play with me."

"See that park over there? I had a birthday party there once. We had a big cake to eat, and after we ate it, we played a lot of running games like sack races and relay races, and then I threw–up—*everywhere*. No, I think they have cleaned it up by now."

"See that big building over there? I spent more time in that building than anywhere else. It's the library. I went there to escape, to think, and to get smarter."

ME: "Well, do you believe I was once a child, *now*?"
THREE-YEAR-OLD: "Did you really get into trouble, Daddy?"

6

BONDING

- *Parent's Bed*

- *Bathing with the Children*

- *Up on My Shoulders*

- *Sleeping Together*

- *Backyard Camping*

- *Weekend Breakfasts*

- *Parents on the Floor*

- *Tickling*

- *Treats*

- *Busyday*

- *Conversations on the Toilet*

- *Taking Walks*

- *Pat-A-Cake*

- *Story on the Back*

When we provide for our children's basic requirements of food, clothing, and shelter, we would best be called their guardians or custodians. Not until we intellectually, emotionally, and physically give and take with our children—or bond—should we accept the title of parents.

The bridge to parenthood is not particularly difficult to build; it just requires some genuine time, energy, and knowledge that the blueprints and materials often hide from us.

Those blueprints and materials can be found in the private domains of the master bedroom and bathroom, the tranquil state of going to sleep and waking up, the inexpressive anatomy of shoulders and back, the ordinary activities of cooking and walking, and most importantly, in the underused sense of touch.

While the bridge is under construction, your investment will come together, growing sturdy. Your children will begin to see you as something more than a provider of their basic needs; they will see you as someone who wants to be involved with them. Then after the bridge is complete, it will serve as a fluid pathway of communication between you and your children for a lifetime.

. . . Wave them into your bed and suspend time.

47. Parent's Bed   *"Different Kind of Intimacy"*

When I was a small child, my parents discouraged me from entering their bedroom, unless it was absolutely necessary. I sensed necessary meant that, at a minimum, a nuclear strike had to be imminent. I was almost sure their attitude stemmed from fear that I might catch them watching cartoons. Of course, as I got older I realized their embarrassment was over their appetite for—you know—*The Three Stooges*.

The physical barrier my parents erected translated into a communication barrier, and a reduction of intimacy—the intimacy between parent and child.

When Saturday or Sunday rolls around and you don't have to be dressed to be somewhere to do something, resist the urge to get out of bed. Instead, wait for your children to arise. (This has been known to happen in reverse.) When you see their spirited grins peeking around your bedroom door, wave them into your bed and suspend time. This unique setting presents the perfect climate for bonding, as everyone is:

1. Refreshed from a good night's sleep.
2. Casual, with no clothes, hair, or make-up to mess up.
3. Comfortable and warm.
4. Removed from the distractions of the world.
5. Physically accessible.

These elements, combined with a childproof environment, set the stage for active play such as tickling, wrestling, pillow fighting, rolling, giggling, hiding. Passive activities include cuddling, stroking, tummy sitting, hugging, and snuggling. Thoughtful conversation involves planning the day's activities, solving problems, or providing reassurance after a difficult night's sleep or bad dream.

Lolling about in bed is a family endeavor often overlooked, because it is so simple as to be a virtual non–activity.

Don't let this fool you, though. It's as strong and everlasting as BEDrock.

48. Weekend Breakfasts   *"Get up—Shower—Dress . . ."*

"Jane, stop this crazy thiiiiing!!!" Whenever I watch George Jetson trying to escape the perpetual motion of his treadmill at the end of each episode, I think he should be able to simply get off it, but he can't.

Our family used to share the same predicament as George, on a constant treadmill, trying to escape its clutches, or at least shut it down now and then. Get up, shower, dress, eat, go to school, go to work, do errands, eat, finish chores, sleep, get up, shower, dresseatschoolworkerrandeatchoressleepgetupshowergetupshower . . . "Honey, stop this crazy thiiiiing!!!" Each day ran into the next, until one was indistinguishable from another. The endless pattern continued until we introduced, developed, then legislated the "Sunday Morning Pancake Breakfast."

No one sets an alarm. No one asks, "What time is it?" No schedule, no plans, no people to see. The treadmill grinds to a halt for much of the morning, highlighted by a leisurely breakfast prepared by the children and me, with the kitchen off-limits to Mom (including cleanup).

The children stand on chairs, helping grease skillets, crack eggs, pour milk, mix pancakes, and sometimes, spill, overflow, tip over, and break. (I didn't say it was the *perfect* Sunday morning pancake breakfast.) I give the kids as much responsibility as possible, without tempting the fates of kitchen dangers. They revel in creating a satisfying meal with—as they see it—dubious ingredients and fire. Using countless utensils, they probe, pick up, turnover, slide, and pat. Crackling, hissing, gurgling, and sizzling sounds reach a crescendo, preceding four or five pleasurable aromas that fill the kitchen. The meal is unrushed, and digestion gets some quality time.

Every part of this custom is contrary to the daily repetition (certainly the quality of the meal doesn't repeat itself), and so the event acts as a counterbalance and re-energizer.

The treadmill can be brought to a halt in many ways. Certainly my solution works wonders at our house, and maybe someday George Jetson will show up for Sunday breakfast.

49. Conversations on the Toilet   *"By the Book"*

"Daddy, come here." From the reverberating sound and direction of the request, I was certain it was coming from the bathroom. I had no doubt my child wanted company while he sat on the toilet.

As I recall from basic psychology, Freud made it clear that to handle the early toilet experiences in any way other than "LY"; sensitiveLY, patientLY, and attentiveLY—would be the equivalent to producing an anxiety-ridden, anal-retentive child.

"Coming, Son." (Why take any chances?)

Conversely, I could challenge Freud's approach, and go by the book with one child and *not open* the book with the other, to see if Freud was correct. Then again, with the threat of children suing their parents, I think I'll pass. Now, although I can't recall my own early toilet experiences, I can imagine that a child's vivid imagination magnifies what is already a very anxious and insecure time.

As I entered the bathroom I leaned against the wall, looked into my son's eyes, and sensed what he was thinking:

What if I fall in? What if I get sucked down the toilet when I flush? Will an alligator come up the sewer and chomp on my bottom? Should I get rid of something that I still might need—but if I don't, could I explode? I hope this room doesn't get any smaller. What if everyone's gone when I come out? Is that terrible odor coming from me?

So, it isn't surprising I am called on regularly to reduce my child's anxiety. The unique environment of a bathroom, free of distraction, where a child is a captive audience and vulnerable, invites the opportunity to discuss his or her fears, concerns, and needs. We also practice fundamental learning, such as counting and the alphabet. When a "backup" happens, I seize the opportunity to point out the benefits of consuming apples over cookies.

I have also learned something myself from this experience. I now know what the proverb, "Necessity is the mother of invention" means, because I have now learned how to breathe through my mouth.

50. Bathing with the Children   *"Take Note, Cleavers"*

You have to figure that the contentment children receive from taking a warm bath goes back to the security and comfort they received from their nine-month stay in the warm waters of the womb. Add to this bath experience bubbles, imagination, and participative parents, and you have the ingredients of rewarding times with your children.

Baths provide a calming effect before bed, a springboard into a new day, or spontaneous fun in the middle of a cold winter day. The natural and liberating experience facilitates a two-way openness with your children like no other experience can. It initiates the lines of communication between parent and child, and demystifies sexuality. Questions of anatomy are more easily asked and answered without fanfare, and the process of sexual identification begins.

We clean each other, not unlike a family of chimpanzees. This process yields bonding, caring, and reassurance. We play Santa Claus, as bubble bath bubbles become facial hair. We make interesting boats out of shaving cream. We play "Where's the Soap" in the murky water, and giggle at the intestinal bubbles that rise from the cloudy deep. Only our imaginations limit the possibilities of things to do in the tub.

The children secure great byproducts and everyone gets squeaky clean to boot. But the most rewarding aspect of this experience is that our family transcends the flawlessness of the exemplary Cleaver (as in, *Leave It To Beaver*) household, because I have yet to hear the whiny objection, "Do I have to take a bath?"

51. Parents on the Floor   *"Fertile Ground"*

Would you like to decrease the psychological distance and increase the intimacy between you and your children? Of course you would. Then it's time to get eye-to-eye with them, on *their* level Therefore, Mom, get up off the love seat, and Dad, up out of your easy chair. Bend your knees, and keep going until your bottom has bottomed out onto the floor.

As soon as you do, you will observe a transformation in your children. Their expressions, their posture, their attitude, all exude eagerness and anticipation from your "visit."

What occurs from that point forward is up to you and them. There is no right or wrong way to fulfill the experience. Just let it happen—and it will. Here are 18 games we repeat, because of their popularity:

• Horsy	• Wrestling	• Face Anatomy
• Staring	• Ball Rolling	• Choo-Choo Train
• Helicopter	• Steam Rolling	• Marco Polo
• Tickling	• Under the Bridge	• Flip Me Over
• Make a Letter	• Bucking Bronco	• Boo in the Blanket
• What Animal Am I?	• Pile It Higher	• Make a Muscle

Some of these activities' names probably make sense. I'm sure others appear puzzling. I will leave it up to you; I am sure your imagination is every bit as good as mine. It doesn't matter what you do—just that you do it. Take even a traditional activity such as reading, and move it down to the floor; you will find it greatly enhanced.

Let's face it, sitting in furniture and standing on the floor are largely restrictive and one-dimensional. Conversely, the floor has no boundaries or presumptions. It is fertile ground for parents and children to become physical, impulsive, and close.

52. Taking Walks   *"A Foreign Country"*

The preschool child's world does not extend much farther than his or her house and yard. When children venture beyond those boundaries, their experiences are not much different from ours, the first time in a foreign country.

The child's world is fixed, routine, and structured. Children see virtually the same things, in the same places, day in and day out: their rooms, clothes, toys, dining areas, views out the windows, bathrooms, and so on. Mealtimes, rest times, bedtimes, and regimens occur at roughly the same time every day. Not much is extraordinary; not many surprises occur.

Just the opposite becomes true, however, when we take a walk. The children are completely out of their element, then. Much of the experience is random, unexpected, and rarely routine. The walk provides a setting for educating, socializing, communicating, and exercising. The children get to experience some independence by making decisions such as:

1. What to take along (food, water, sweater)
2. Where to go (store, friend's house, vacant lot, around the block)
3. What direction to take (left, right, straight)
4. How fast to travel (fast, slow, stop)

We see a person we don't know, and I talk to the children about strangers. We stop and talk to a neighbor we *do* know, and they learn social skills. They come upon a new dog and learn caution. They see a car speed by, and learn the importance of looking before crossing.

A worker repairs utility lines, and the children learn how water and electricity get into our home. A bird prepares its nest, and they learn about nature and the importance of respecting all living things.

Their questions, concerns, and disappointments come about more readily when they are away from the house, out in an environment of free association. Additionally, their physical development and health get a boost from the demands of the walk.

Walking, a simple, but often forgotten activity, is an ideal way to ease your children from *their* world, into *our* world.

53. Up on My Shoulders   *"Déjà Vu"*

"Eat all your vegetables and you will grow big and tall like this," I suggested, as I hoisted my youngest child up on my shoulders. I heard only hysterical laughter as my child reacted to the new adult perspective (or to the balding spot on the crown of my head).

Rarely do children have such an opportunity to see, manipulate, maneuver, and experience the world as we do, at our level. With this in mind, help them enjoy our point of view, so they can:

EXAMINE: The whites of our eyes (instead of the underside of our chins) ✦ Brownies baking in the *upper* oven ✦ The other side of the fence ✦ Who's in the picture on the fireplace mantel ✦ What the large crowd is looking at ✦ What the Pharmacist is doing.

MANIPULATE: The items on high shelves and in cabinets at home ✦ The light bulbs in or out of a socket ✦ A basketball into the basket ✦ The fruit from a tree ✦ The food items on the high shelves at the market.

RIDE: To bed at night ✦ To greet people at the door ✦ Around the neighborhood for a walk ✦ In a circle as a lighthouse beam ✦ Around in the swimming pool.

Of course, with this broadening of horizons can come potential *headaches*, so . . .

WATCH OUT FOR: Door jambs ✦ Low-hanging branches ✦ Hanging lights ✦ Clotheslines ✦ Ceiling fans (especially those in motion).

The seemingly trivial amusement of raising your child up on your shoulders might have even greater significance as a metaphor for validating your child. The contrast of being *up* versus *down* is worth examining.

- To LIFT your children up is to INSPIRE.
- To SUPPORT is to ENCOURAGE.
- To ELEVATE is to give PROMINENCE.
- To make them HIGH is to EXCITE.

Conversely . . .

- To keep them DOWN is to OPPRESS.
- To let them DOWN is to DISAPPOINT.
- To look DOWN on them is to HUMILIATE.
- To be DOWN is to be DEPRESSED.

You might imagine that someday, when your children are grown UP, they might stop in their tracks and experience a contented feeling of déjà vu.

54. Tickling   *"Contaminated Sensitivity Powder"*

What was Mother Nature thinking when she gave us the capability to be tickled? Is this sense really necessary for survival? Has anyone ever been tickled to death? Maybe when she was mixing up the ingredients for the skin, she got a bad batch of "sensitivity powder," and ticklishness was the result. Or maybe, because we can't tickle ourselves, ticklishness was her way of encouraging social interaction, like incorporating, we couldn't tell ourselves a joke and laugh.

When humans are deprived of tactile stimulation, they're emotionally affected, which gives substance to my theory. Whatever the reasons, one thing is for sure: children can't get enough "tickle episodes." (Nevertheless, remember to keep the duration of each episode to a minimum.) An infant immediately responds positively to, "This little piggy went to market." Tickling children in the right spots often causes hysterical laughter—yet they will continue to come back for more.

- The palm of the hand — How long can they withstand?
- Above the knee — They just might pee.
- Under the arm — Don't get alarmed.
- On the side — They might just divide.
- Bottom of the feet — Can they take the heat?

Heck, just *tell* them you are going to tickle them, and they will come undone. However trivial this horseplay appears, it often can work well as a communication bridge. Here are 10 times when you might find it useful and fun to tickle your children. When:

1. You want to wake them up.
2. They won't tell you what's wrong.
3. Violence appears in a TV show (to distract them).
4. They are bored.
5. You want to extract a confession (good naturedly).
6. You want to find out if they really hurt themselves badly.
7. They are angry.
8. You are washing them in the bathtub (no intent required).
9. They are sad.
10. They have the hiccups.

Remember, make sure that when they tickle *you* for the first time, you bite your lip and say convincingly, "I have never been ticklish." This performance will make the rest of your life much easier.

55. Pat-A-Cake   *"Just Like, I Love Lucy"*

Pat-a-cake, pat-a-cake, baker's man
Bake me a cake as fast as you can
Roll it, and prick it, and mark it with a "B"
And put it in the oven for Baby and me

Next to "Happy Birthday," "Pat-A-Cake" might one of the more recognizable and performed songs around. Well, maybe *song* isn't the proper classification—at least the way I deliver it. Maybe a nursery rhyme? Then again, maybe not. I haven't seen it in any books, and it's not violent like, "Jack and Jill," or scary like, "Little Miss Muffet," or gloomy like "Old Mother Hubbard." Maybe a sonnet? How about a limerick? Possibly a poem? No, I don't believe it's any of those.

Anyway, I do know one thing, that word for word (just 38), it is one of the most entertaining verses for children. That's it, verses! And unlike "Happy Birthday," you can recite it more than once a year! So what makes this very short composition such a crowd pleaser with the children?

1. The elapsed time fits well with a child's attention span.
2. The words are short (no word over six letters) and simple.
3. The subject is food. A high priority on a child's list—and about cake no less!
4. The simple rhyming cadence. (You can ask Dr. Seuss about this.)
5. The physical closeness includes sitting on your lap and clapping hands.
6. The camp-song style combining gestures with vocals (*roll it and prick it*).

Ironically, the song's simple nature becomes more enduring rather than boring, with each recitation. Maybe it is analogous to our response at seeing the same *I Love Lucy* episode, for the 18th time—the comfort of constancy. No doubt there are cynics among us who just can't accept that anything in life can be so innocent and pure. I can hear them now:

"Babies can't have cake; it's solid food. So who is it really for?"

"Why mark the cake? Is there contraband in it? A file, maybe?"

"What's the hurry? A prison break?"

"Why did the baker's man (or flunky) bake it, and not the baker himself? Is he on the take?"

Because we really don't know whether a conspiracy is afoot or not, let's keep it to ourselves and let the children have their Pat-a-cake—and eat it, too.

56. Sleeping Together   *"Without Hesitation"*

Recently, my son had a spontaneous episode of inappropriate behavior. Translation: He was in BIG trouble. So we gave him a choice between two punishments. One choice was to forfeit playing with his friend that day—a friend he had been asking to play with all week. The other was to forfeit our Friday night ritual of sleeping together in our sleeping bags. Without hesitation, he chose to forgo the rendezvous with his friend.

His choice surprised us a little. You might think after three years of crawling into our sleeping bags every Friday, the ritual would have lost some of its luster and novelty. When I put myself in his place, however, I realized that this ritual fulfilled some of his fundamental needs—needs more fragile and amplified in adolescence. Here are some of the more predominant ones.

- SECURITY: As I recall my childhood memories of nighttime, the darkness and quiet were unsettling and forbidding, exposing insecurities and vulnerabilities.

- ANTICIPATION: Expectation is sometimes more exciting than the event itself.

- RECOGNITION: He gets my full, undivided attention for the evening, with no competition from other family members.

- SELF-ESTEEM: Because it's *his* night, he gets to steer the rudder. He chooses which book to read, what game to play, what to talk about, even when to go to sleep.

- LOVE: I believe the ritual itself communicates devotion and caring for him that can't be duplicated in words. The logic for him might go something like this:

"If Dad is willing to sleep in a sleeping bag on a hard floor with me, rather than under a down comforter in a soft bed with Mom, then he must really love me."

57. Treats   *"Less Is More"*

The first words out of my children's mouths when I walk in the door from work, aren't, "Daddy, Daddy, we missed you!" or "Look what I made in school today!" It's "TREAT! TREAT! Did you bring us a treat?"

If I did, I'm the best daddy in the world; if not, call Social Services and have me reported for child cruelty. This isn't a case of spoiled children expecting a new bike, train, or rocking horse. The expectation is more along the lines of a marble, Life Saver candy, decal, or stick of gum. (Even a shiny rock I picked up in the yard once did the trick.)

Since this is such a big deal to the children, I added some variety to enhance the moments when they shout, "TREAT? TREAT?" Some past examples:

1. "Which hand?" I held out two closed fists.

2. "I have a treat, but you have to find it. It's somewhere on me," I teased. They delved into my pockets, shoes, socks, collar, until they located it.

3. "I don't know . . . I don't remember." I smiled deviously and proceeded to the bedroom to change my clothes, but I didn't get far. "I'm not sure where it is. Maybe it's over there." I diverted their attention. When they looked away, I threw their treat in the air and then looked as surprised, as they did, when it hit the ground.

How can this nominal trifle bring as much, if not more excitement and enjoyment, than an expensive birthday gift? Maybe it's because:

1. "It's the thought that counts," really *does* count.
2. It's a random event elevated by anticipation that builds with time.
3. There are no expectations, like there are at holidays and birthdays.
4. The event gets associated with Dad being home. (Which is certainly cause for celebration, isn't it?)

Maybe the reason is really very simple, transcending logic and analysis, captured by Robert Browning, who said, "Less is more."

58. Story on the Back   *"Creeping Spider Named Kay"*

Our backs are almost like strangers to us. We don't see them much, touch them often, or pay a great deal of attention to them. Despite this neglect, they dutifully follow us around wherever we go. Maybe that's why when we feel the hot sun baking it, a hot shower surging on it, firm hands massaging it, or gentle finger-tips brushing across it, we check-out of reality, and into serenity.

As you may have noticed, children too, have backs. Why not, then, provide them with a like experience? You can even enrich it with cerebral and bonding elements. Here is how to proceed: Pick out one finger, from one of your hands. Place it on your child's back. Now push your imagination in high gear. You will now tell a story on his or her back, leaving your child to fill in the missing pieces of the story.

Here is an example to get you started:

Legend: CAPITALIZED items indicate motions, letters, or numbers to perform on the back; parenthetical items are what your child will solve to move the story along.

Once upon a time there was a SLITHERING (snake) named B (Bea), a HOPPING (frog) named J (Jay), and a CREEPING (spider) named K (Kay). "Y (Why) don't U (you) come 2 (to) my place 4 (for) a bar B (be) Q (cue)," said B (Bea). "I'll prepare your favorite bugs for the main course, with PPP (peas) on the side, and M&M's 4 (for) dessert. We can watch TV and play T–ball 4 (for) fun."

J (Jay) the HOPPING (frog) said, "G (Gee), that would B (be) fun."

K (Kay) the CREEPING (spider) said, "Sure, I'll C (see) U (you) after my I (eye) doctor appointment."

Unfortunately, what was 2 (to) B (be) a day of fun turned into a nightmare 4 (for) all. First, J (Jay) the HOPPING (frog), and K (Kay), the CREEPING (spider), made B (Bea) the SLITHERING (snake) angry by taunting, "We 1 (won) at T–ball." Then they made B (Bea) angrier by criticizing, "PU! These PPP (peas) don't smell right." 2 (To) make matters worse, some little boy took a pot shot with his H2O (water) gun, at B (Bea) the SLITHERING (snake). The final draw came when the 2 (two) guests exclaimed that there wasn't enough food 2 (to) eat. B (Bea), the SLITHERING (snake), agreed, and proceeded 2 (to) make a B–line for J (Jay) and K (Kay) with his jaws wide open.

"EEE! O (Oh) no, U (you) R (are) not going 2 (to) eat us, R (are) U (you)?" K (Kay) exclaimed. With that, B (Bea) the SLITHERING (snake), 8 (ate) J (Jay) and K (Kay) in 1 (one) big gulp. From that day on, B (Bea) regretted that meal, because of the bad stomach ache it gave her with TICK-LING (chills), TICKLING (shivers), and TICKLING (shakes), that never went away.

59. Backyard Camping   *"Darn Porch Light"*

"OK, kids, follow me. Watch out for that obstacle, there. It's just a little farther. Now stay close. No, not that way, the terrain's too rugged! How about this spot, right here? OK, you can drop your stuff. You know what? Go tell Mommy to turn off the back porch light, please, so we can see the moon better."

OK, so we didn't rough it in the wilderness. Put me in a home for wimpy dads, if you must. Nevertheless, before you pass judgment, consider that backyard camping has many of the same benefits of the wilderness experience, without the fuss and muss. Just the right amount of time and trouble for the young ones.

To best illustrate the attraction of this recreation, here is a comparison by way of the senses of the typical indoor routine versus the exceptional outdoor adventure.

SIGHT: Moon vs. Nightlight ✦ Stars vs. Four Walls ✦ Clouds vs. Ceiling ✦ Limitless vs. Enclosed

HEARING: Breeze Ruffling Trees vs. Flushing Toilet ✦ Crickets vs. Clocks ✦ Crackle of Hibachi Campfire vs. TV ✦ Silence vs. Settling and Creaking

SMELL: Honey Suckle Blossoms vs. Dirty Clothes ✦ Grass Fragrance vs. Post-Meal Kitchen ✦ Smoky Aroma vs. Bathroom Odors ✦ Sausage vs. Stale Air

TOUCH: Soft Flannel Sleeping Bag vs. Matted Polyester Blanket ✦ Parent's Caress vs. Tattered Stuffed Animal ✦ Campfire Warmth vs. Central Heating ✦ Supple Grass vs. Crusty Carpet

TASTE: Juicy, Open-Fire Hot Dogs vs. Microwaving ✦ Hot Gooey Marshmallows vs. Out of the Bag Cold ✦ Fire-Crisp Bacon vs. Soggy, Greasy, Fried Bacon ✦ Runny Egg vs. Runny Egg (Well, three out of four isn't bad. Besides, food just tastes better outdoors.)

True, the camping adventure is not on a mountain or in a national park, on a lake or near a river, at a YMCA or in a scout camp, but it certainly is in, and will remain in, the hearts and minds of your children forever.

60. Busyday   *"Tie a Ribbon"*

What started out as an innocent question right before I kissed my children good night, "Did you have a busy day today?" has turned into a special nighttime ritual called appropriately enough, "Busyday." The children turned the adjective and noun combination into a noun. Now, after story time, they remind me, "Busyday! Busyday!"

No doubt a child's day—relatively comparable to an adult's week—is busy. No time for coffee breaks. No time to sun themselves. A child just has two speeds: Go and asleep. Nevertheless, between go and asleep, after the lights go out, are five to ten minutes of precious time available to wrap up the day and tie a ribbon around it. Here's a typical interchange and its value.

DAD: "Did you learn anything in preschool today?"
YOUNGEST: "Yes, not to talk with strangers."
VALUE — A dialogue begins about this important matter.

DAD: "I liked that you helped your mother with setting the table this morning."
OLDEST: "You did?"
VALUE — Attention for doing something positive.

DAD: "What did you do today that was the most fun, and what was the least fun?"
OLDEST: "Playing the guitar was the most fun; making me stop was the least fun."
VALUE — New awareness of an interest in music.

DAD: "It seems like something is bothering you."
YOUNGEST: "A boy pushed me at school."
VALUE — It shows trust and allows for solutions.

DAD: "Do you feel bad about anything you did today?"
OLDEST: "I accidentally flushed a ball down the toilet."
VALUE — Keep your patience, increasing the chance for future honesty.

DAD: "Wow! You're going to play at the park tomorrow."
OLDEST: "I can't wait."
VALUE — Anticipation is half the fun.

Sure, some Busydays yield nothing of great value. Even so, they still provide a good transition to sleep time, the stability and security any ritual gives, and the signal to them you care about their day. Is the value of the childrens' day diminished if they fall asleep during story time and miss out on Busyday? Probably not. To the contrary, I figure they flaked out because they *had* a busy day, and there is certainly some value in that.

7

CREATIVITY

- *Cardboard Boxes*

- *Toilet Paper Cylinders*

- *Pencil and Paper*

- *Board Paintings*

- *Sidewalk Chalk*

- *Sand*

- *Paper Airplanes*

When children, or anyone for that matter, are creating (i.e. painting, building, drawing), their demeanor changes dramatically. They become calm, focused, and at peace, possibly as a result of the mind escaping the captivity of routine and habit. The benefit of this process is as valuable as the tangible product created, if not more so.

When children create something, they make profound progress toward their development. They build their identities, focus on their capabilities, and make friends based on common interests.

Children sometimes think that there are only two ways to do something, right and wrong (probably perceiving emphasis is on wrong), so the creation process must appear refreshing. No rules. No structure. No judging. No right or wrong.

Parents can make a big difference by encouraging their children to create, and praising their children for the resultant product, and not only for the reasons given above. Many creations (products, art, inventions, performances, and so on), that some people consider of questionable quality succeed in the world. Conversely, many possibly terrific products never see the light of day. How does such injustice occur?

Let me ask you this: Have you encouraged and praised your child lately?

. . . Place a box inside a wrapped box and DOUBLE their pleasure.

61. Cardboard Boxes   *"Imagination Inside"*

So you can't think of any presents to give to your children for the next gift-giving occasion? Well, how about a fort, a robot, a train, a storage container, a house, a basketball hoop, a tunnel, and a pet house. If you think the sum of these purchases is a little out of your budget range, think again. Can you afford wrapping paper and cardboard boxes? Of course you can. Proceed to your local rental store and purchase assorted boxes in a range of sizes. Wrap them up—fill one or two with a little imagination—and you have showered your children with all these gifts and more.

1. Turn over a large box, and children have their own private fort.
2. Cut holes for windows and doors, dress it up with crayons and paint, and they have a house.
3. Place a few well-chosen holes in a medium-size box, color it, and your child can become a robot.
4. String together small boxes, and create the little "boxcar" train that could.
5. Provide shoe boxes as containers for all their little toys (cars, blocks, balls, dolls, toy soldiers).
6. Place a large box on its side and provide the catalyst for make-believe worlds of school house, fire station, restaurant, hospital, and so on.
7. Put a medium box against the wall to make a basketball hoop, challenging early coordination, where any object is fair game in an attempt to make two points.
8. Put long rectangular boxes end to end to fabricate a tunnel.
9. Place food and bedding in a small box as a temporary home for a surprise house guest (lizard, frog, caterpillar).
10. Give your children the best birthday present ever; place a box inside a wrapped box and DOUBLE their pleasure.

Without a doubt, the cost-to-playtime ratio of boxes is second to none. Nevertheless, as with any apparently perfect scenario, there is always a downside. Prepare for the possibility that one day your children might have to buy a house twice the size than they might otherwise need; enough for their belongings *and* all the boxes that they came in.

62. Board Paintings   *"Long Italian Surname"*

How much of your childhood artwork, such as drawings, paintings, and paste-ups, do your parents still possess? Probably up to about—none. Chances are your inspired creations decomposed, became fertilizer, assisted in tree growth, and was processed into paper, that your children now use for *their* artwork.

Oh, I guess your mom could have saved your productions in a box after their time came to leave the spotlight of the refrigerator or bulletin board, but what would be the point? Assuming you could locate the box, what kind of crippled state would the artwork be in, a generation later?

Wouldn't it be a treat, for nostalgia and conversation's sake, to have a few of those mementos from your childhood? It sure "wood" and I do mean wood. You know, the building material derived from trees, just a little higher up the byproduct ladder than paper. Well, it's too late for you, but not for your children. Wood is a perfect surface on which to create a lasting piece of art. You know those scrap pieces of plywood and boards in the basement you've been saving to build that birdhouse or end table? Face it; it's never going to happen.

Instead, give the scrap wood in its present state to your children, along with paints and tools, and let nature and instincts take their course. Children can use oil paint, watercolors, or even house paint. They can apply them with paintbrushes, toothbrushes, hairbrushes, or toilet brushes. They can apply them with sticks, Q-tips, sponges, or rags. When the prize art is complete, hang it in a prominent place where it won't get lost, and will virtually last forever.

"Hang it in my home?" you say. Well, sure. Why, pay for a pretentious painting that has great value only because the painter is dead, when you can cherish a creative expression of your own flesh? If you are self-conscious, you can probably pass the artwork off to visitors as a "_____ original" (fill in the blank with a long Italian surname). Tell visitors you had to mortgage the house for the painting.

Besides, maybe Clement Greenberg was right when he said, "All profoundly original art looks ugly at first."

63. Sand   *"Universal Language"*

What significant object in the world works only because it is disintegrated, worn, and broken? What substance would be noticeably absent, leaving us without cement, glass, and computer microchips? What item is so abundant, its number is compared to stars in the universe? What element fills our oceans, lakes, rivers, deserts, playgrounds, and backyard _____boxes? What can help give life to vegetation, or bring death by quick_____, and help keep track of the time by way of an hourglass? Give up? Bullies often use *it* to shame and intimidate 98 pound weaklings. A body of this material can provide hours of recreation for children. Yes, sand! (I knew this last clue would give it away.)

Place 100 children in the middle of a sand pile, and chances are 99 would still be playing there one hour later. (One may have to leave to get a booster shot.) What will children do in a sand pile? Give them:

1.   A bucket, and they will build castles.
2.   A stick, and they will draw and write.
3.   A sifter, and they will examine all foreign substances.
4.   A dump truck, and they will move it around.
5.   A shovel, and they will dig holes and tunnels.
6.   A BIG shovel, and they will build forts and bury each other.
7.   A magnet, and they will collect iron.
8.   Toy soldiers, and they will fashion a battlefield.
9.   Toy cars, and they will construct a race course.
10. Nothing, and their hands and fingers will create and invent.

Place 10 children from 10 different countries in sand together, and they all speak the same language; the universal language of Sand. The only uses as yet undiscovered for this abundant and versatile matter would be to fuel our automobiles or to cure cancer.

I guess someday this resource might be used for so many purposes that it becomes scarce. Then my worst fear could be realized: The sandman could be without his magic to help put my children to sleep.

64. Toilet Paper Cylinders   *"Many Roles"*

"We're all out of toilet paper!" I yelled from the bathroom. The universal euphemism for: I am captive here until someone brings me a new roll. Almost instantaneously, I heard the quickening of footsteps as they grew louder. That is service.

The door flew open. "Can we have the toilet paper roll?" the winded children eagerly begged.

"Here, but could you . . . " Gone, before I could finish my sentence.

Whether it's an empty roll of toilet paper, paper towels, tin foil, or wrapping paper, disposable cylinders still have a long and useful life as important make-believe props and amusements. Here are some items to MAKE, and the *ROLES* that accompany them. Make a:

1. PERISCOPE (two with tape) and be a *SUBMARINE COMMANDER.*
2. LOG CABIN (many with glue) and be a *PIONEER.*
3. PENCIL HOLDER (paper-plate bottom) and be a *WRITER.*
4. BINOCULARS (two with an ice-cream stick in the middle) and be a *SPY.*
5. TELESCOPE (Two with 2 different diameters) and be an *ASTRONOMER* or a *PIRATE.*
6. MEGAPHONE (string around neck) and be a *COACH.*
7. BIRDFEEDER (plate & hole) and be a *NATURALIST.*
8. MOLD (fill with sand) and be a *CASTLE BUILDER.*
9. PRIVATE PAPERS CARRIER (string as a handle) and be a *SECRET AGENT.*
10. BULLET TRAIN (10-foot string) and be an *ENGINEER.*
11. BUG CATCHER (put a hole in it) and be a *TRAPPER.*
12. STORAGE ORGANIZER (five to seven vertical, with paper plates) and be *EFFICIENT.*
13. FLYING CYLINDER (paint it and fling it) and be an *AERODYNAMICIST.*
14. HOLIDAY ORNAMENT (paint and string) and be a *DECORATOR.*
15. LONG PIPE (many tubes with tape, roll a ball through it) and be a *PHYSICIST.*
16. BAT (draw it brown or black) and be *BABE RUTH.*
17. BARBER POLE (red, white, and blue paint) and be a *STYLIST.*

Then, when the holidays roll around, make the empty WRAPPING PAPER ROLL a gift, and be a *HERO.*

65. Sidewalk Chalk   *"The Setback Age"*

When I drove up to the house, my children practically laid down in front of the car, blocking the entrance to the driveway. (I think they decided they have had enough, and didn't want me around anymore.) Then I discovered they had covered the driveway with artwork using their "blackboard chalk on steroids," chalk sometimes called, sidewalk chalk. It made me ponder whether we might someday see the following headline:

DATELINE: JUNE 14, 3710: CIVILIZATION REGRESSES. A new period of man was discovered today by archeologists. It is being termed the "Setback Age," because of its primitive form of communication that clearly is a step backwards from previous technological civilizations. The era has been dated between 2000 A.D. and 2500 A.D.

Found fossilized in concrete, somewhere in what used to be North America, were representations of primitive stick people, purple dinosaurs, numbers, and letters, all which appear to be a form of communication. The colorful pictures and writings are believed to have been made from fossilized shells that make a chalky, powdery, limestone substance. Clearly, this age is a large setback from the period that immediately preceded it, the "Silicon Chip Age."

For all we know, what was termed Egyptian hieroglyphics, representing some of the earliest communication, might really have been done by a bunch of kids playing in a cave. Whether in a cave, or on a patio, street, sidewalk, or driveway, sidewalk chalk allows children to imagine and create in the fresh air, on a large scale, with no boundaries, and no cleanup.

The children draw animals, faces, lines, circles, letters, numbers, trees, water, and you name it. When they run out of ideas, I might intervene and help them draw hopscotch squares or a path to ride bikes, a line for a standing broad jump, an imaginary tightrope to walk, a circle in which to throw beanbags, the outlines of a mosaic to fill in, a foursquare for ball playing, or squiggles to start a picture. When the children tire of entertaining themselves, they offer, for a small gratuity, to draw a special picture on the neighbor's driveway. They draw pictures for the people passing over in airplanes, for nothing, and attract friends over to play by offering to draw them, for their company.

Sooner or later, Mother Nature passes by, and as I tell my children, "Spots the beautiful artwork below, and unable to hold back the tears, cries in response, washing it all away. At first she is sad, but then realizes she can come by again to behold a whole new series of beautiful work created by beautiful children."

66. Paper Airplanes   *"Folds and Gravity"*

Throw a flimsy piece of paper. Nothing happens, right? It probably didn't get much farther than your feet. Roll it up into a ball and do the same thing. It goes a few feet farther, but so what? Now, make a few strategic folds with it and let it fly. Bank to the left, dive, level out, smooth landing! It could have glided over 1 1/4 miles, which, if it did, would be the new outdoor paper airplane distance record.

Wow! Paper, a few folds, and gravity, and you're in for an afternoon of aviation fun. Here are a few ideas to enhance your flights of fancy:

- CONSTRUCT: Draw the lines where you want the folds to go. This process enables your child the pleasure of making the three-dimensional plane.

- ART: Almost as much fun as flying it, is coloring it. Your child will need no help here. Pilots, windows, markings, engines, flames, wheels, his or her name, and more. (When flying is over, make a mobile and hang it in your child's room.)

- CONTESTS: Go for distance off the raised patio deck, or from the ground. Mark the spot with chalk, and see if the distance can be bettered. Fly the plane through a hoop or a tire. Try to land it within a large circle, or in a wastepaper basket. Get the neighborhood kids to compete.

- EXPERIMENT: Try different aerodynamic designs. Some work better than others. Teach your child the concept that the more time and effort put into a task, the better the chances are to succeed.

- MAKE-BELIEVE: Your child can play "airport," and draw runways, terminals, and the control tower with chalk. He or she can be pilots, flight attendants, air traffic controllers, or passengers. Your child can have fighter aircraft go on missions, track down the enemy, get into dogfights, and take care of the enemy. For a special effect, YOU can set one on fire, and have it "crash and burn." Then play "rescue," with your child by being a firefighter, policemen, or nurse. Fly to Grandma's house to visit her.

- EXERCISE: You crafted aircraft, and not boomerangs. Therefore, your child will be good and tired after chasing them down all day, and will be in bed early.

Nevertheless, don't expect to pick up that novel you're trying to finish after your child goes to bed. Instead, you'll be creasing paper, getting ready for the next day's flights.

67. Pencil and Paper   *"A New Discovery"*

They were once made of lead, but are now made of pure china clay, graphite, and cedar from 150 to 200-year-old-trees. Their companion, once made from linen and cotton rags, is now made of wood pulp. If I could provide only two material objects to my children, outside the basic necessities, it just might be pencil and paper.

For CHILDREN they can provide these five benefits:
Entertainment ✦ Creation ✦ Learning ✦ Therapy ✦ Relaxation

PARENTS derive these five benefits as a byproduct:
Pride ✦ Insight ✦ Solitude ✦ Interaction ✦ Observation

Gliding over the blank paper are the hand and pencil together, translating intangible imagination and thoughts into the tangible. The pencil acts as the voice of the movement, and paper the receiver, ostensibly making concrete what the mind intended. Nothing more pure, and pencil and paper require no setup or instruction, while their use offers no right and no wrong.

My son is amused at the dog he has drawn. (ENTERTAINMENT.) Mom looks over his shoulder and is impressed that the picture is better proportioned and more defined than in his past drawings. (CREATION.) "That's really neat, son. Let's put it up on the wall." (PRIDE.)

Mom goes back to drinking her coffee. She takes a deep breath and becomes conscious of the birds chirping outside. (SOLITUDE.) Her attention turns again toward her son. She is touched by his quiet demeanor. (OBSERVATION.) He is serene and focused, with tongue out, seemingly to help guide his hand. (RELAXATION.)

"Why don't we practice your letters and numbers? (LEARNING.) We can play Hangman for letters and Dot-to-Dot for numbers. (INTERACTION.) When we're done, we can do that game where I draw the squiggle and you make a picture from it."

"No, I want to finish this," he exclaims. Mom observes a picture of an angry person. "Is that *you* with the scowl on your face?" (INSIGHT.)

"I'm mad at Daddy for getting mad at me today," he says while he broods. "Come here; let's talk about it," Mom comforts. (THERAPY.)

With the arrival of computers and electronic communication, pencil and paper may eventually vanish. Nevertheless, I'm optimistic that a future civilization will invent a device to assist in creating and communicating, one that's easy to learn and operate, at nominal cost, which requires no electricity, and has 100 percent reliability. We can only hope after they *discover* pencil and paper, they won't disappear again.

8

NATURE

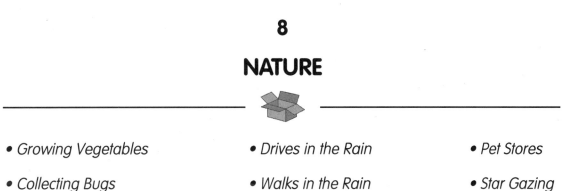

- *Growing Vegetables*
- *Collecting Bugs*

- *Drives in the Rain*
- *Walks in the Rain*

- *Pet Stores*
- *Star Gazing*

Nature and your child are a lot alike: If you completely ignore them, they will remind you of their presence, in not-so-kind a way. Your child will tug on your shirttail, then kick you in the shin. Nature will often warn of her delicate balance, and may someday rebelliously kick the planet out from under us.

We often take for granted and fail to appreciate the silent world of nature. Its beauty and splendor masked by our busy routine and day-to-day responsibilities. Unless a butterfly lands on our shoulder, or nature's fury impacts us personally, we usually don't pay much attention.

With our children in our shadows, however, the time has come to tune in with our senses and conscience, and introduce them—and us—to all of nature's textures and flavors. Without heads full of adult clutter, children find it much easier to respond to a flower blooming, a star shining, an ant working, or a raindrop falling, with innocence and awe.

The awareness of nature's activities will serve to inject qualities of humility, sensitivity, nurturing, and responsibility into your children.

Furthermore, when your children are ready to make their way in the world, their interaction with Mother Nature may inspire them to pursue such related occupations, such as veterinarian, botanist, geologist, astronomer, or meteorologist.

Who knows? Someday your child may help with the responsibility of keeping Mother Nature from kicking the planet out from under us.

. . . A speck of green on a background of brown.

68. Growing Vegetables   *"Mud into Carrots"*

"I see it, I see it!" my children screamed while bending over the planter full of dirt. In unison, the rest of us bent over and squinted. They were right; a speck of green on a background of brown, the first indication that the carrots were—or at least one carrot was—growing. Predictably, their next words were, "Can we eat it now?" The answer, of course, disappointed them.

Despite their skepticism when I told them if they planted seeds in fertilized dirt and watered them they would grow into carrots, the children dutifully watered them every day for two weeks. Consequently, they were rewarded with a microscopic green speck and eventually a completed specimen. To my children I'm a prophet, and they are magicians! *Well we must be*, they surmise, *to turn mud into carrots, by pouring water onto dirt.* Don't underestimate the power of such a seemingly insignificant activity. It contains the nourishment and some of life's fundamental lessons for children, such as the following:

- INFLUENCE: They recognize they are not completely passive beings; that they have the capacity to affect the world around them.

- SELF-ESTEEM: They have the opportunity to accomplish a task that appears difficult to them, thereby building their confidence to undertake future challenges.

- RESPONSIBILITY: They learn that their actions have consequences, positive or negative, and they can be held accountable for them.

- RETURN ON INVESTMENT: They learn there is a relationship between the time and effort put into a task, and the success that is realized.

- NATURE: They begin an introduction to the ecosystem, the complexity of nature, and the interrelationship of all living organisms.

69. Drives in the Rain   *"Clear—Fuzzy—Clear"*

The randomness of the weather must be extremely mysterious to a child. Snow, rain, wind, thunder, lightning, clouds, sunshine, and so on, come unpredictably and in varying degrees. We compound the intrigue when we shrug our shoulders in response to our child's question as to what the weather is going to be on any given day. Yes, we *can* quote the forecast, but we really don't know for sure. Adults too, are intrigued by the weather, treating it as a novelty. They often begin conversations with it, comment on it as it occurs, and even watch it on television, where it has its own channel!

Like an involuntary reflex, the children usually scurry to the window at the first sound of raindrops on the roof. Although apprehensive, they don't want to be passive bystanders, so they shout, "Can we go in the car?" This is their way of being daring.

Once in the safe bubble of the automobile, they relax. They are silent for a while, as they absorb the sounds and sights of the elements outside: rain pelting the roof of the car, windshield wipers making the terrain look clear—then fuzzy—then clear, tires splashing water at different intervals and pitch, and thunder ominously rumbling.

Then the questions come. "Why is it raining? Where does the rain go? When will it stop? What if it never rains again? Can we drink the water?"

When I tire of answering questions, I ask them what *they* think. I try to avoid the answer, "just because" (although sometimes they wear me down like a tenacious lawyer, and I can't help it).

Suffice it to say, this adventure sharpens children's imaginations, observations, and knowledge, and rivals any nature show on television. At times it even provides peace and serenity.

When the adventure is over and we pull into the driveway, the children disembark, examine the vehicle, and beam with pride that they survived the experience, safe and sound.

70. Pet Stores *"Check for a Pulse"*

If while strolling at the mall, you are able to pass by a pet store without stopping at the window or going in, then check to see if you have a pulse. If you can pass by when your children are with you, forget the pulse—check to see if you have a heart.

Whether you view these stores as an exploitation of animals for commercial gain or an invaluable service for both man and beast, it's hard not to, "oooooo" and "ahhhhh." So have a heart, and introduce your kids to *theirs*. Enter the store, and enjoy the safari. You can even show off to your children how much you know about the animal kingdom.

1. Pet the velvety fur of the RABBITS. Watch them snuggle, never blink, and explain to your children that their constant nose twitching means they think you smell funny.

2. Observe your heart rate slow and a sense of calm come over you while following the perpetual motion of the FISH. (Why do you think pediatricians' offices have aquariums?) Explain that the neon fish have a small battery and light bulb inside them.

3. Howl at the CATS sparring, batting, and good naturedly antagonizing each other. Explain to your children that *they*, too, act just like that.

4. Interact with the BIRDS by conversing with the PARROT, shushing the PARAKEETS, and asking the proprietor to place the COCKATIEL on your shoulder.

5. Apprehensively watch the REPTILES, and note the contrast in their movements: the laboring TURTLE, the rapid-tongued SNAKE, the almost motionless IGUANA. Explain that the snake doesn't have bones because he doesn't drink his milk.

6. As the GERBILS hyperactively scurry on their wheel to nowhere, explain that although they could light up a city of fifty thousand people, this fruitless activity is what happens when you eat too much sugar.

Communicate and bond with the DOGS in various ways: Pet them, and they become still; scratch their bellies, and they're all yours. Remark, "What a pretty puppy," and watch their eyes brighten and tails wag. Put your face up close to theirs, and chances are they will lick it. At that moment you'll know you have a heart.

71. Collecting Bugs   *"No Mayonnaise Please"*

I'm ashamed to admit that when I was a youngster, I wasn't exactly a defender of the bug and insect kingdom. Ants, snails, grasshoppers, and worms scurried under large leaves on the ground when I came around. With a magnifying glass, honey, salt, and firecrackers at my disposal, I was Public Enemy #1, to the insect world.

Nevertheless, in retrospect, I thought I was pretty well adjusted, as were my friends who did essentially the same things. We were just being *boys*. That was mischief, well within societal bounds, right? In contrast to what the *bad* boys were doing (the same thing we were doing only to parents and teachers probably), it seemed pretty benign.

Now, I know we weren't just being mischievous; we weren't just being boys; and we weren't well within societal bounds. What we *were* being was insensitive, ignorant, and just plain cruel.

When I was young, no one taught me the principle that we should respect all living organisms. No one explained to me that animals and insects play an important role on our planet, benefiting mankind. No one pointed out that killing or torturing defenseless creatures, no matter how small, was cowardly and senseless. Well, that moral neglect would change when it came to my children.

"Kids, go get me a mayonnaise jar, preferably empty," I requested as my children stalked a caterpillar. I found the best approach to teach my children was to lead by example.

We punched a few holes in the lid (don't forget that part), and collected a variety of bugs and insects (grasshoppers, beetles, moths, spiders, caterpillars, ladybugs, ants, worms). We observed them, fed them, read about them in the encyclopedia, and then returned them to their habitat. I never had to utter the words "respect," "important role," or "benefit mankind." My children got the message through actions.

If you doubt this method is effective, then please note that the last time my son observed a bug crawling across the driveway, instead of stepping on it, he bolted to the house to retrieve a mayonnaise jar.

72. Walks in the Rain   *"We Are Waterproof"*

A difference of opinion exists as to whether it is a good idea to go walking in the rain. Gene Kelly, lovers on the movie screen, and children all seem to think it's a wonderful notion. Conversely, the Wicked Witch of the West, the Tin Woodman, and mothers, generally oppose this activity on the grounds that one might melt, rust, or catch a cold, respectively.

Although the controversy may never be resolved, I generally support the activity, for humans, anyway. For one thing, I think mothers are heavily influenced by commercials where kids come in out of the rain sniffling, and then given cold remedies to make them feel better. How do our bodies know what type of water they are coming in contact with, anyway? We don't get colds from bath, pool, or shower water, do we? Furthermore, I have been outside in the rain without an umbrella many times and have never rusted, malfunctioned, or short circuited. Clearly, we must be waterproof.

Rain is a large part of our lives. It's a staple of casual conversation and always on the newscast. It feeds our earth, and dictates our outdoor pleasures. It has inspired hundreds of songs, and contributed to many catastrophes. A mysticism surrounds it, especially for children: Millions of water drops descend from somewhere; don't know when it will start; don't know when it will end; don't know how much will come down, or if it will turn to snow.

The liquid attracts children to build dams in the street gutters and catch it in a cup to measure it, run in and out of it from the garage and float a leaf in it down the street, catch it in their mouths and do a rain dance to bring more.

Sometimes they prefer to be in it and not get wet by wearing a raincoat, holding up an umbrella, or getting in the doghouse.

Oftentimes, enough satisfaction is gained by searching for rainbows, identifying figures and forms in the clouds, and splashing in the puddles.

After the children and I exploited all the possibilities of the rain, we headed toward the warmth and comfort of the house. As Mom stood in the doorway awaiting our entrance, I recognized the moment as one where my children could benefit from my years of wisdom. I bent over, put my arms around them, and whispered, "Don't sniffle, or we're all dead."

73. Star Gazing   *"They're Not Moving"*

To a child, adventuring beyond his or her home and yard, and into the neighborhood, might be the equivalent of you and me traveling to a foreign country. The neighborhood greatly expands your child's world, as a foreign country would do for us.

Given this context, what can we say about journeying out to the stars and planets, so to speak, with the naked eye or a telescope? The expansion is literally out of this world, for both a child and an adult. For a child, however, it might be a little more overwhelming, amazing, maybe even frightening. Nevertheless, don't let it stop you from initiating or encouraging a discussion about astronomy, though. In fact, go outside with your child on a crystal clear evening and begin a dialogue. It might go like this:

DAD: "Did you know there are more stars than grains of sand?"

SON: "How many more?"

DAD: ". . . and the stars are so far away and moving so fast, you are seeing them as they were millions of years ago."

SON: "Huh? I'm seeing them right now, and they're not moving."

DAD: "No I mean . . . the light takes . . . well, the closest star, besides the sun is over four light years away. Did you know it would take billions of years for me to drive there, going 55 miles per hour?"

SON: "What if Mommy drives? Will we get there faster? Can we go there now?"

DAD: "No, but we can look through a telescope and see the stars as if they were much closer. A powerful telescope can see a candle burning 100,000 miles away."

SON: (pointing) "Is the candle on *that* star?"

DAD: "No. That's the moon, and there is no candle on it, but astronauts traveled there and landed."

SON: "How can they land on it if it's moving so fast?"

DAD: "Well, they . . . they . . . well the moon and stars *do* move! Some believe a really fast-moving asteroid, which is like a star, crashed into the earth, ultimately causing the dinosaurs to become extinct."

SON: (concerned) "Not Dino though. Do the Jetsons live up there?"

DAD: "Yeah. They live in the Big Dipper. Little Elroy goes to the Little Dipper School, right? See up there? See those seven stars? Connect them, like you do when you play Connect the Dots and you'll see a dipper."

SON: "How do I connect them? . . . Dad, you look like you're mad at me. Why does that star sparkle?"

DAD: "Uumm, well . . . well, how could they have written that song, 'Twinkle, Twinkle, Little Star,' if it didn't?"

DAD & SON: (Singing together) *"Twinkle, twinkle, little star, how I wonder where you are. Up above the world . . . "*

Well, given enough time, you can always find some common ground.

9

EXPRESSION

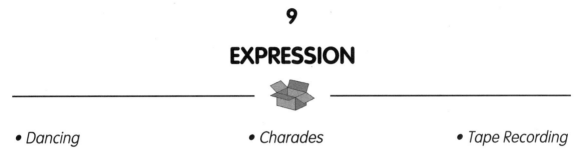

• Dancing   • Charades   • Tape Recording

• Singing

Quite often the individual's need for expression is in conflict with society's expectations. Children have a need to express themselves, primitively and impulsively at times, as an aid to maximize their potential. Their raw spirits, however, must be tempered for us to function as a viable society. Unfortunately, the socialization process often over-tempers this need, leaving children short-changed.

Parents, often uncomfortable with their own alter egos, unwittingly discourage their children's expression. For example, they positively reinforce quiet and sometimes withdrawn behavior from children by remarking, "Oh, they're just shy."

Remember, how petrified you were as a child, at having to get up and speak in front of the class? Remember how scared you were at your first dance? These public displays may still be difficult for you, contributing to missed opportunities and potential fulfillment.

Now with a perspective, however, you have the opportunity to minimize the stress of potentially traumatic events for your children. Encourage their expression in a "safe" environment, where you can participate with them, and positively validate their expression.

They will subtly develop self-confidence and self-acceptance and, who knows, you just might become a little less shy, yourself.

... *You are not a parent, and they are not children.*

74. Dancing   *"Not a Parent or Child"*

Whenever the stereo played, my 17-month-old began to grin and bounce up and down. Surely this must be an inborn response, not unlike crawling, walking, and little boys missing the toilet. Play your favorite rhythmic music and see if you observe the same results. Instantaneously, a silly grin should come over your child's face, followed closely by his or her unsuspecting torso involuntarily bouncing up and down to the beat. No coaxing is necessary. It is truly a Kodak moment.

There is something missing from this picture, however. You! From here on out, especially during the children's toddler years, they will receive great pleasure from dancing (and I use that term loosely) to the music, and even greater pleasure when you participate. I know what you're saying: "I'm far too dignified to dance with my children. My children will lose respect for my authority. I lost this inborn response you referred to sometime between birth and my first junior high school dance." No, you're not. No, they won't. No, you didn't. Even if you were right on all counts, the joy you and your children will attain by your participation will far outweigh your embarrassment and presumed damage to your ego. Think back to how you felt when your parents participated with you in something you loved to do. Let that feeling guide your actions here.

Now get out to the middle of the family room floor with your children, and turn up the volume. Twirl, twist, swing, bob, spin, swim, monkey, hustle, shake, rattle, and roll. If you and children aren't soon laughing hysterically, then I would hold a mirror to their noses to see if they're still breathing. They won't notice your awkward movements and clumsy footwork, only your love for them.

After a while, you'll forget what you look like or just won't care because of the look you see on your children's faces. In addition to all the fun you'll have, you'll also get your recommended daily dose of aerobic exercise. The most profound observation you can make from this pastime, however, is that for a brief time you are not a parent, and they are not children, and there has to be something special about that.

75. Charades   *"Silly and Profound"*

Question: What particular event contributes to our growth by opening up communication, expanding our thinking, uninhibiting us, encouraging role playing, providing insights to personality, bringing us closer to people, and building our confidence?

If you said a productive session at the psychologist, you get partial credit. If you said, however, a carefree game of party charades, you score full credit. Furthermore, if you suggested that party charades could be altered and played as family charades, then you get extra credit and are hereby authorized to add 50 points to your SAT scores. Your children can also enjoy the same benefits. Here are some suggested categories more appropriately designed for the younger members of the household:

1. Favorite TV personalities (Barney the dinosaur, Bart Simpson, Bugs Bunny)
2. Family Members (Dad, brother, Grandpa)
3. Bad Habits (picking nose, chewing with mouth open, sticking tongue out)
4. Animals (cow, duck, bear)
5. Future Events (new baby, time for bed, vacation place)
6. Daily routine (brushing teeth, taking bath, getting dressed)
7. Family activities (eating dinner out, grocery shopping, going to a movie)
8. Backyard activities (throwing a ball, going down the slide, playing in the sand)
9. Indoor activities (blocks, trains, reading)
10. School activities (finger painting, cutting with scissors, singing)

All children are creative in their own ways, but many never have a chance to demonstrate it. Charades provides a secure environment to have that opportunity.

If a picture is worth a thousand words, then so are the gestures exhibited in this game. Parents might gain some insight into their children's behavior and motivations. Children might see a more human dimension of their parents. Parents and children share a common denominator, while playing this game.

It is a silly diversion, but it's also a profound requirement. Yes, it's two—two—two games in one.

76. Tape Recording   *"Squabble Extinguisher"*

Remarkably, the most effective method I have found to extinguish a squabble between my children is not a threat or a punishment, but the introduction of a thin plastic-coated layer of iron and chromium flowing through the coils of an electromagnet.

"Who wants to hear themselves on the tape recorder?" I loudly interjected. Instantaneously, my children stopped in mid-quarrel, and came to attention in anticipation of the red light, that indicated the recorder was taping.

What special powers does this electronic gadget have that I don't? Could it be its capacity to give the children an out-of-body type experience? Might it be the children's natural proclivity to be narcissistic? Or maybe it's just the magic of it. Fortunately, I don't have to know the cause to reap the rewards, so I just sit back and watch it break up squabbles, and capture my children's focus and imagination.

Moreover, I think some subtle value is attributable to the seemingly frivolous pastime, even though scientific evidence is lacking. It exercises creativity, increases self-awareness, reinforces memory and verbal skills with counting, reading, and singing, and helps children pronounce words correctly, by hearing them played back.

Yes, the tape recorder employs a wonderful technology, but like any useful body of knowledge, there is always the potential for it to backfire. With this in mind, it probably wouldn't hurt to share with them the story about a man named Nixon.

77. Singing   *"Couch and Underwear"*

Singing is a recreation almost all of us can do, but few of us do well. Because we don't do it well, we do it, rarely. We do it in the shower, because no one is around, and we sound amazing. We do it at places of worship, because *everyone's* around, and no one can tell we don't sound quite so amazing. We do it while driving alone in our car, where generally no one notices or cares.

I'm sorry, but this isn't quite good enough. It's time to abandon your pride and self-consciousness, and sing along with your child. I don't mean burst out in show tunes, with three part harmonies backed by a 50-piece orchestra. I mean, sit on the couch, in your underwear, singing: *"Flintstones, meet the Flintstones. They're the modern stone age family. From the, town of . . . "*

It doesn't matter what you sing, where you sing, how you sing, or why you sing—just sing. Television sitcom themes, traditional children's songs, commercial jingles, sixties surfing tunes, nursery rhymes, camp ditties, Lithuanian work songs, whatever. If you or your child know the words, then the song is a candidate.

Yes, I know it is tough to peel off this layer of yourself; nevertheless, after a time, you will forget you are tone deaf. Other people around won't, but you won't care. You and your child will be having a ball. Just keep singing and remind all those with their hands over their ears, that your child is profiting in the following 10 ways:

1. Expressing personalities
2. Improving memorization
3. Bettering moods
4. Becoming more extroverted
5. Banking fond memories
6. Bonding with parents
7. Expressing joy
8. Improving verbal skills
9. Developing music appreciation
10. Expending energy

" . . . Bedrock. They're a page right out of history. Let's ride, with the family down the street . . . "

It's tough to stop, once you get started.

10

INTELLECT

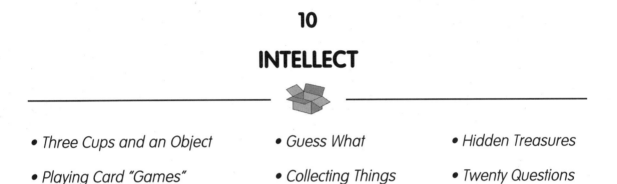

- *Three Cups and an Object*
- *Guess What*
- *Hidden Treasures*
- *Playing Card "Games"*
- *Collecting Things*
- *Twenty Questions*

If we use less than 10 percent of our brains, as science has told us, you have to ask yourself: How can this be? Homo sapiens has been around for 300,000 years, which is certainly ample time for the brain to have evolved to its full potential. Could television have retarded its progress? Could our schools be letting us down? Could the other 90 percent be filled with advertising jingles?

It's hard to answer these questions with less than 10 percent of my brain, so I won't try. Nevertheless, the amusements highlighted in this chapter will contribute toward stirring up some of the virginal gray matter. Skills such as observation, deduction, reason, and organization will begin to take shape. The indentations and crevasses of the brain will begin to show the effect of learning and thinking—I think.

The sequence will go something like this: The delight your child will express when he or she guesses the correct answer will warm your heart. The positive reinforcement you provide will accelerate learning. Then finally, the chance for some future generation to eventually claim 100 percent brain utilization will take a giant step forward.

. . . For as long as your arms—or the M&M's—hold out.

78. Three Cups and an Object *"M&M's and Crickets"*

(Back and forth, back and forth, switch hands, around and around, switch hands, STOP.)

"OK. Which cup?" I asked.

"That one!" my oldest exclaimed.

(Lifting the cup)

"Not it," I asserted.

"That one!" my youngest said with assurance.

(I lift the cup.) A single, yellow M&M is revealed.

"*EEEEEE!* I want to eat it!"

"No, me!"

"The one who guesses right gets to eat it," I explained.

So it went until the package was all gone. Little preparation was needed and not much skill was required. If you can find three cups that look alike—not transparent—and an object that is smaller—not larger—than the cups, you are on your way to capturing your children's attention for as long as your arms—or the M&M's—hold out. If the activity catches on, variations abound, some of which are even educational. Here are some of the variations:

1. Use pennies. (The children keep the money for their piggy banks.)
2. Use Scrabble letters. (Have them spell words with the tiles.)
3. Use numbers. (Have the children put them in order, after they find them.)
4. Distract the children. (Hide the object in your shirt pocket and amaze them.)
5. Be sneaky and put one object in every cup. (Worth the double blink and surprised look.)
6. Keep the object in your hand. (Take it out of their ear.)
7. Use a piece of sponge. (Wet it and tell them it grows under the cup.)
8. Use raisins. (Provide some nutritional value to offset M&M binge.)
9. Substitute. (Show them an M&M; have them discover a peanut.)
10. Try for consecutive correct guesses. (Grant a reward.)

When the children's attention wanders, it is time to involve Mom. After being left out of all the fun, she can't wait to be asked. After you have played for a while with the children, using the M&M's, invite her over to participate. Go through the routine and ask, "Which cup?" Eventually she will point to the cup that you have previously tampered with—the one you put the LIVE cricket under! (Life just doesn't get much better than this.)

79. Guess What *"The Subordinate Senses"*

One of the earliest recollections of my life, was of my father coming home from work, standing bigger than life in front of me, and announcing, "Close your eyes and put out your hands." A chill went through me even if he dropped nothing more than a stick of gum or a Life Saver in them. Trying to guess the surprise gave me an additional thrill.

Unless we are blind, our sight tends to overpower our other senses: hearing, taste, smell, and touch. Sight diminishes other sensitivities and lessens our enjoyment of them. If you have any question in your mind, close your eyes and LISTEN to the rain fall, STROKE your spouse's face, TASTE a bite of your favorite dessert, and SMELL bread baking in the oven.

Now combine for your children the excitement of guessing and surprises with the stimulation of the four subordinate senses, and you've fashioned a game with infinite possibilities. Have your children close their eyes and guess a particular sound, smell, taste, or texture. Of course, you will probably find some senses are more developed than others at their tender age. Do you recognize some of these indicators?

- HEARING: Poor. (How many times do you have to tell them something?)
- TASTE: Good. (Highly discriminating. They reject more food than they accept.)
- TOUCH: Good. (Highly ticklish.)
- SMELL: Poor. (They seem to *enjoy* passing gas.)

Here is how to play the game: Have the children close their eyes, or better yet, put a blindfold on them. Remember how good you were at keeping your eyes closed at the game Marco Polo? Place objects in their mouths, under their noses, in their hands, and near their ears. Here are some ideas to get you started:

- HEARING—zipper, keys, stapler, biting into an apple, opening a soft drink.
- TASTE—raspberry, M&M, vanilla extract, butter, pancake (no syrup).
- TOUCH—stuffed animal, can opener, battery, clock, dollar, hair brush, sponge.
- SMELL—peanut butter, dirty sock, soap, their blankets, lemon.

Just one word of warning, though. Try not to mix up the objects with the senses; touching peanut butter, or tasting a dirty sock, doesn't work quite as well.

80. Hidden Treasures   *"Sans Mr. Bunny"*

Next to Christmas, probably the next most magical and exhilarating moment a child in a Christian family experiences is finding hidden eggs on Easter Sunday. The adrenaline that flows at the anticipation of finding them, and the explosive surge of pure happiness when he or she finds them, makes merely thinking about an egg hunt as vivid as the real thing.

So why limit your children to this feeling just once a year? No, you don't need to summon the Easter Bunny to your home once a week, like we once did the milkman. There are some everyday ways to give your children that "hidden eggs" feeling, sans Mr. Bunny.

You can, for instance, draw a picture of something they really want, such as a piece of cake, toy car, or stuffed animal. Cut the picture into four squares and hide the pieces around the house. When they are all retrieved, the children get the actual reward.

You can buy a nominal trinket they really want and place it under a box. Add a number of empty boxes (maybe10) around it. Tell them that when you spot them being, or doing something good, they can pick a box. If they pick an empty box, they have increased their chances the next time. As you will find out, B. F. Skinner was right about motivating good behavior with random positive reinforcement. Here are more ideas you don't need Mr. Bunny for:

1. Are you ready to take a break from the children? Break open a roll of pennies and scatter them all over the backyard. "No, that's only 47. You have three to go."

2. When siblings are fighting over something, it's game time. Hide the item and the first to find it, gets it. (Right, make it impossible.)

3. Are the children fighting over who will help mix the cake batter and who will frost the cake? Hide the items and, well, you get the idea.

4. Hide a number of different objects under boxes. Let them see you hide them. Then ask them which box an object is under. (Somewhat like the game show *Concentration*.)

Hide a ticking clock, and *hear* it out. Hide a fresh brownie, and sniff it out. Hide a particular book, and read it to them when they find it. You are only limited by your imagination.

And Mr. Bunny, you don't have to worry; you will still have a job once a year.

81. Playing Card "Games"   *"The Learning Irony"*

Often, the best learning takes place when we are not attempting to learn at all. It might occur when we are enjoying a hobby. It might take place when we are reading. It might happen when we are playing a game.

With this in mind, open a deck of simple playing cards and play some "games." When you are finished, your children will have learned: basic memory, counting, number recognition, mathematics, logic, observation, and probability, all by "sleight of hand." Just execute a few shuffles, and they will come running. Here is how to teach—by not teaching at all:

1. MEMORY: Turn over five or six pairs of cards (lay them out in the shape of a house, airplane, and so on). Have the children turn over two cards at a time to try to match them. If the cards don't match, turn them back over. When a match is achieved, put them aside.

2. COUNTING: Give the children some cards and ask, "How many red cards?" (Or black cards, hearts, spades, face cards, jokers.)

3. NUMBER RECOGNITION: Play the card game, War. Split the deck in half. Each child turns over a card, and the highest card takes both cards. Play until one has all the cards.

4. MATHEMATICS: "What does this card (a 3), plus this card (a 5), equal?"

5. LOGIC: Place cards upside down, in a circle, in numerical order. Turn one over (for example, a 2). Ask the child the card number four cards up (a 6).

6. OBSERVATION: Play, Three-Card Monty. (Use three cards, face-down, one a queen. Shift around the cards and have the children tell you where the queen is.

7. OBSERVATION: Play, "Which One Is Different." The kings, queens, and jacks all have some commonality and differences. Have the children figure out the differences, for example one king has only one eye; one queen is facing a different way; one jack has a mustache.

8. PROBABILITY: Play, In Between. Show two cards, for example, a 2 and a 10. Ask them whether the next card will fall in between or not.

When your offspring have mastered all these challenges, they have one left to meet. Have them learn the number 100. By building a house of cards with that many stories, they will break the world's record. You might want to attempt this feat outside, because it will end up being 19 feet high!

82. Collecting Things   *"Especially Gains"*

Rocks, bottle caps, sports cards, shells, comic books, marbles, matchbox cars, coins, stamps, dolls, posters, buttons, pins, stickers, autographs, hats, post cards, model planes, butterflies, and so on.

Almost any item that isn't nailed down or too heavy to lift is a candidate for collecting. Just about everyone, at some time in life, has collected *something*. The phenomenon is strange if you think about it. The activity basically involves finding the items, organizing them, counting them, storing them away, looking for more, and then doing it all again—and again, and again. The activity is often addictive, and it never has an end. So . . . why?

Could the caveman's hunt-and-store instinct still be with us? Is collecting merely a healthy outlet for a long obsolete drive? If so, then we have been duped, and should probably discourage collecting in our children, so eventually the evolution of it will phase out. Right? Wrong!

Too many valuable benefits are byproducts of collecting, and besides, who are we to play God? Here are some of the profits your children can collect:

1. They find a focus of their boundless energies that could have been channeled less constructively.
2. They are given a very simple and basic challenge (rocks, stamps, shells, and such), whereby a child can succeed.
3. They earn a feeling of pride.
4. They create a characteristic that sets them apart from others.
5. They find a means to interact with and make friends.
6. They receive a lesson in negotiating and compromising, when trading such as with baseball cards or stamps.
7. They learn a lesson in counting. ("I have 53 rocks now!")
8. They get a lesson in categorizing and organizing.
9. They have a reason to take care of, and appreciate, a possession.

You will reap a benefit too. Someday, because you encouraged them to start a collection, they will accumulate, then auction off a valuable one. Out of appreciation, they will give you the proceeds so you can retire. (Right.)

83. Twenty Questions *"A Natural"*

What do children do best? Not listen? Yes, they are pretty good at that. Avoid going to sleep? They do that well, too. Cry? They have that down to an art. Asking questions? Bingo! That's the one.

Questions come out of their mouths like machine-gun fire. Why? Where? When? How? Who? What? Is it? Can it? Will it?

You really can't blame them. They're curious and want to learn. You attempt to answer faithfully, and construct a thoughtful answer each and every time. After another round of questioning, however, you break down like a weary witness on the stand. "OK, OK, the sky is blue because God had an over-supply of blue crayons! *Boo-hoo-hoo-hoo.*"

Why not take advantage of what they do best. Channel this natural curiosity, cultivate it, and even enjoy it, and play Twenty Questions. (Or 138 questions, if they need it.) Here is how the game might go:

CHOOSE AN OBJECT in the room (in this case the TV) and say, "OK, I'm thinking of something." Then, here come the questions:

"Is it bigger than you? Is it yellow? Is it near the couch? Is it lower than the shelf? Is it on the floor? Is it brown? Do we turn it on? It's the TV!" my child deduced correctly.

Twenty Questions PASSES TIME on a long car ride. "OK, I'm thinking of something. Can you guess what it is?"

"Is it outside? Is it in the back seat? Is it in the front? Is it close to Daddy? Does it move? The steering wheel!"
"No, Son."
"Is it high up? Is it black? The flipper thing!"
"Right, the visor," I corrected.

It can take some time before the children catch on to the game, but once they do, it's in their blood. Also, when *they* get to pick the object, they become highly excited, because how often do they know something you don't know? The game of Twenty Questions increases their basic skills of observation, problem solving, questioning, and logic.

One day before long, when your child is in the questions asking mood and inquires, "How come you have *one*, Daddy, and Mommy doesn't?" you'll know just what to do. Look around the room and say, "OK, I'm thinking of something . . . . "

11

COORDINATION

- *Ball on a String*
- *Hands and Fingers*
- *Flipping Cards*

- *Scissors, Paper, and Paste*
- *Mimicking*

- *High Jump and Limbo*
- *Home Bowling*

Just what is coordination? We know it's the complex synchronization that occurs when we demonstrate mastery of our bodies, but what *really* is it, and how does it work? OK, I'll try to explain.

One hundred thirty million light-sensitive cells in our eyes inform our minds, with 100 trillion nerve connections, to command our bodies with 206 bones, and over 650 muscles, in a continuous, simultaneous loop, to accomplish such things as hands moving effortlessly across the piano, the body moving precisely through a gymnastics balance-beam routine, juggling to keep multiple balls in the air at one time, and high diving acrobatics through the air and hitting the water in exactly the precise pose.

Although society appreciates and admires athletic achievements, many people complain that too much emphasis is placed on physical feats at the expense of intellectual accomplishments. Maybe this is so; however, our children's pride, esteem, and acceptance often come more, from how they perform on the playground, than how they perform in the classroom.

Don't dismay. Find ways to nurture this different kind of intellect called coordination. Maybe the confidence your children gain from mastering their bodies can be applied someday to their effort in discovering a cure for cancer.

Shelbyville-Shelby County
Public Library

. . . *Hung by twine, in each car stall.*

84. Ball on a String   *"The Sports Center"*

For the longest time, we couldn't park our cars in the garage. Most people struggle with getting organized from time to time, so our clutter shouldn't seem surprising. Tools, garden equipment, toys, and junk reproduce like fungus, spreading throughout the garage. In my case, however, the tools are always in the basement, the garden equipment always in the shed, and the toys and junk are regularly sent off to charity, when they have outlived their usefulness. In fact, my garage floor is virtually disinfected.

What's the problem, then? Well, what stands between the garage and my cars are two tennis balls, hung by twine, in each car stall. "Come again?" you say. That's right. Their function is to take the guesswork out of determining where to stop the cars when we pull into the garage. When the windshield makes contact with the ball, the engine goes off. *"Apparently, I have missed something. Please elaborate."*

Well, with little appreciation or understanding of the purpose of these devices, the children have turned the hanging balls into a sports center, badgering us to leave the cars outside, so they can use them. When the children play, I observe components of baseball, tennis, handball, and tetherball, all built into a singular apparatus.

- With a baseball bat: *CRACK!* — a three-bagger down the 3rd base line.
- With a tennis racket: *BOOM!* — a forehand winner, cross-court.
- With their hand: *SMACK!* — palm to the ball, then off the wall.
- With two children: *SLAP! SLAP! SLAP!* — back and forth like a tetherball.

It's probably just a matter of time before a commercial on television will tout: "PLAY ALONE OR WITH A FRIEND! THE ALL AMERICAN, ALL-IN-ONE, ALL-SPORTS BALL! ONLY $29.95! Some assembly required."

As a result, I have assembled two more balls on a string. They hang under my patio deck for my children, and allow me to return my cars to their rightful places in the garage.

85. Scissors, Paper, and Paste   *"No Single Letters"*

It is raining outside, and inside three children bounce off the walls, which is frustrating your effort to get the house in order. In three minutes, the pastor's wife who heads the, "Are You a Fit Wife and Mother Committee" is scheduled to arrive for a social call. The floor is a mess with old magazines, snapshots, and sheets of paper spread all over. Additionally, oldest child (A) has to make a family photo collage for a school project. Middle child (B) must do his homework, which consists of demonstrating his knowledge of the letter sound, M. Last, but not least, youngest child (C) is living life and couldn't care less what problems you might have. Now quickly, with three minutes to act, which course of action do you take?

   A. You panic, become immobile, and hope for divine intervention.

   B. You calmly walk out the door, never to return.

   C. You contemplate switching to atheism.

   D. You grab scissors and paste from the cabinet, pick up old magazines, snapshots, and paper from the floor, and put them all on the kitchen table. You instruct child (A) to cut out pictures of his family from the snapshots, paste them on the paper, to make his collage. You instruct child (B) to cut out magazine pictures that start with the letter M. You tell child (C) to merely cut away to his heart's content. (Time elapsed: 1 min. 38 sec.)

Although the right answer is B, I suspect most of you chose the parentally responsible, politically correct answer of D.

   The beauty of cutting and pasting is it's easy to get the activity going, and there is little limitation to what the children can create. You have a use for your old magazines, your children's attention span increases, and there is little maintenance on your part, including minimal supervision and mess. Still, here's are a few DO's and DON'Ts to keep in mind:

DO: Cut out a mask from construction paper, and then draw a face.
DON'T: Give your children photographs of your spouse's old flame to cut up.

DO: Encourage scissors' use, to develop hand strength and hand-eye coordination.
DON'T: Let them use Daddy's old magazines, which he cherishes.

DO: Have contests such as who can find, then cut out a specific picture from a magazine first.
DON'T: Let the children give the house pet a haircut.

DO: Let them draw a spaceship, cut it out, then play make–believe.
DON'T: Let them cut up a winning lottery ticket.

DO: Advocate cutting up junk mail.
DON'T: Promote cutting out of single letters from magazines. *
(* This may be how serial killers get their start.)

86. High Jump and Limbo   *"Javier and Dennis"*

"High Jump and Limbo." Yes, it could be the title of a new detective series on television. It would probably star Javier Sotomayor, the world's high jump record holder at 8 feet 1/2 inches, and Dennis Walston, the world's Limbo record holder at 6 inches. (6 inches!) The pilot episode would have Javier and Dennis chasing down a would-be suspect by jumping over—and going under—cars trapped in an L. A. traffic jam.

"High Jump and Limbo," however, is not a detective show, but are two basic athletic endeavors, human challenges that carry remarkable records that are testaments to our species' capabilities.

The equipment is the same for both: Some boxes and a broomstick do just fine. The object is also the same for both: Pass the vertical plane of the bar without knocking it off.

The similarity ends there, however. It's:

1. High versus low
2. Explosion versus control
3. Over versus under
4. Strength versus flexibility
5. Bend versus roll (or flop, dive, hurdle, and scissors)
6. Run, jump, and fall versus creep

As an added benefit, these activities prepare your child for many varied careers, including the following:

FIREFIGHTER:
- SHIMMY under the smoke level, where oxygen still exists.
- JUMP over burning debris.

ARTIST:
- BEND backwards to paint chapel domes, such as the Sistine.
- HURDLE pews after an angry mob deems the ceiling obscene.

PLUMBER:
- SQUEEZE under cupboards to fix leaking pipes.
- VAULT over furniture to leave customer's home after a bill disagreement.

EXTERMINATOR:
- BEND low under houses to spot termites.
- LEAP high to clear the large cockroaches.

If your child doesn't quite measure up to the physical demands of these careers, he or she can always take a shot at writing a television series, and I've got the perfect idea . . . .

87. Hands and Fingers   *"Spider Push-ups"*

Hands and fingers and children just seem to go together. (Yes, I know, *everyone* has hands and fingers that go together.) Let me demonstrate with nine CHARACTERISTICS of children and some associated pastimes:

1. Children are curious about HOW THINGS WORK: (Musical Instrument) — Cup hands together with two thumbs facing up, then blow between them. Move fingers of outside hand up and down to play different notes.

2. Children can improve their DEXTERITY: (Finger Control) — Put all fingers together and separate each from one another individually.

3. Children best relate to the SIMPLEST OF PLEASURES: (Spider Pushups on a Mirror) — Put tips of fingers and thumb together, then turn hands sideways. Spread fingers apart and together for the effect.

4. Children love to COPY AND ACCOMPLISH what we do: (Church and Steeple) — Intertwine fingers inward with pointer and little fingers up and tips touching as steeples. Put thumbs together for doors: "Here is the church, here is the steeple, open the door and see all the people." Open hands to reveal all the "people."

5. Children love to be ENTERTAINED: (Ten or eleven fingers?) — Count your fingers to reveal there are 11, not 10—like this:10,9,8,7 . . . SIX, plus FIVE on the other hand equals Eleven.

6. Children like to be able to SHOW OFF to friends: (Half a Finger Gone?) — Face the palm toward the body and bend the pointer finger at the joint.

7. Children WANT OUR TIME and attention: (Let Your Fingers Do the Walking) — Use your pointer and middle fingers like legs and let your imagination take over. (Now *you* can walk all over your kids.)

8. Children have SHORT ATTENTION SPANS: (Two or one Finger Wiggle?) — Put one palm down and one up. Bend middle fingers inward and intertwine hands. Wiggle middle fingers in unison.

9. Children love to be PHYSICAL: (Itsy bitsy spider) — Place tip of thumb against pointer finger of other hand. Rotate hand and touch pointer finger to tip of thumb to other hand. Repeat until the "rain comes down the spout."

Many of these hand amusements have been handed down from past generations. They're a handful to learn, but if you lend your kids a hand, they'll have no trouble handling it. When they have mastered them all, you, of course, give them—a big hand.

88. Mimicking   *"Marcel Marceau or Sheep"*

Didn't Shakespeare say, "To mimic or not to mimic, that is the question"? Well, if he didn't, he should have, because children often have to make the choice of when, and when not to imitate a speech or action, or mimic. You can help your children sort through this dilemma. For example:

Follow the Leader is the preferred game given the choice of playing it, or playing in the storm drain because friend Billy Bingham is. In Follow the Leader, children learn to socialize, concentrate, and follow directions, not to mention that they burn up energy. If a child wants to emulate his friend, Mom might say, "If Billy Bingham jumped off a cliff, would you?"

Playing the game Simon Says is a far more suitable way to mimic a parent than talking back by repeating an order. Simon Says teaches listening and concentration skills. Talking back teaches sitting-in-the-corner skills. At bedtime, Simon Says, "It is time for bed." Sometimes, Simon has more impact than a parent does.

Singing camp songs whereby children copy the motions of the leader like, "If You're Happy and You Know It, Clap Your Hands," or "The Hokey-Pokey," is preferable to repeating the actions and words of a sibling. When I hear my oldest screaming "Stop copying me!" after being mimicked repeatedly, breaking into a chorus of my favorite camp song helps flush the urge from the children's systems.

Playing Mirror in which a child faces you and mirrors your movements might be a good alternative to impersonating a teacher's idiosyncrasy. When playing Mirror children sharpen their hand-eye coordination. When mimicking a teacher, they can sharpen their blackboard writing skills after school.

Children who never learn to guide their own actions could cease to think for themselves. They could end up mimicking everyone else, like sheep in a herd. On the other hand, if children learn how to make the right decisions, they might someday turn their mimicking talent into positive endeavor. Marcel Marceau and Rich Little haven't done too bad, have they?

89. Home Bowling   *"Roll Well or Starve"*

When prehistoric man hurled rocks and heaved boulders at dinosaurs in an attempt to acquire a meal, the projectiles bounced off the animal's armor-like torsos, having no effect. Man found, however, when he *rolled* the orbs at the beast, they often knocked the dinosaurs off their feet—and out. So with that the sport of bowling began.

By the Stone Age, the game had progressed to something closer to our modern-day game, as reflected by what we have observed in the town of Bedrock. The seventeenth century brought the game to America as a nine-pin game. Two hundred years later, it was banned because of gambling, and a tenth pin was added to skirt the ban. Here it was that the term—technicality began.

Recently, six people set a 24-hour marathon record when they knocked down 242,665 pins. No doubt they would have eaten well in prehistoric days.

Bowling is right up a child's alley. (Sorry.) It's easy to understand, it's easy to perform, and the object is to knock things down. It doesn't get any better than that, for children. So get on the ball (sorry again), and scrounge up the equipment necessary to play the game at home. Here are some items you can use for equipment:

PINS: One-liter plastic bottles ✦ Tennis ball or Pringles cans ✦ Plastic cups ✦ Cut-up 2x4s ✦ Soft drink cans ✦ Paper towel rolls ✦ Paper cups (Paint them white and red, and put numbers on them, too.)

BALLS: Softball ✦ Tennis ball ✦ Baseball ✦ Whiffle ball ✦ Soccer ball ✦ Pool ball ✦ Plastic or Rubber balls ✦ Homemade balls (Make a ball from Play-Doh, with finger holes, and let it harden.)

SURFACE: Hardwood ✦ Vinyl Flooring ✦ Carpet ✦ Tile ✦ Cement ✦ Grass ✦ Dirt ✦ Asphalt. (The flatter, harder, longer it is, the better.)

FOUL LINE: Belt ✦ Yardstick ✦ Rope ✦ Masking tape ✦ Paint (Yes, it's important to discern the difference here between indoor and outdoor foul lines.)

PIN SPOTTER & BALL RETURNER: Look in the mirror and introduce yourself.

Hence, set them up and knock them down, make the strikes and avoid the splits, and let the good times roll. (I'm really sorry.)

90. Flipping Cards   *"Wilbur and Orville's Inspiration"*

Give your preschool child a deck of playing cards. Nothing. Give your child a small wastepaper basket. Still nothing. Now give your child both of these at the same time, and stand back.

> FLIP – *SHOOO, SHOOO, SHOOO.* Miss.
> FLIP – *WHOSH, FWAP-FWAP.* Miss.
> FLIP – *FEWWW, FWAP, FEWWW. CLINK.* "Yes! Two points."

With playing cards and a wastebasket, children are entertained for hours, reacting to the unpredictable flight of the cards as they cut through the air like high-tech flying saucers. No one can predict whether a card will go into the receptacle; they defy all aerospace principles.

Seemingly, this pastime is just another trivial diversion for children, however, I understand—although I can't confirm any of it—that this pleasure has quite a history of fable and folklore. For instance:

1. Hoyt Wilhelm, the great knuckleball pitcher, was just another mediocre fastball pitcher, until he applied the principles of this game to perfect his great pitch.

2. On rainy days, Wilbur and Orville worked inside, using this pastime to observe aero principles, and ultimately applied them to their aircraft development.

3. A chapter from one of Hoyle's books, described this game, entitled, *"Cards Not According To Hoyle."*

4. Wham-O, the toy-maker got its inspiration for the Frisbee, from this game.

5. Lewis Carrol? That's right. Rumor has it that this amusement, not mind-altering experimentation, inspired his Queen of Hearts scene in *Alice In Wonderland*.

6. Houdini, because unfortunately he could not master this card skill, chose instead to became a Master of Escape, which ultimately led to his demise.

7. I believe a group of couch potatoes have formed a committee petitioning this sport to become part of the next Olympic Games.

Oh yes, I almost forgot. Dr. Naismith was influenced greatly by the pastime, which inspired him to invent the game of basketball; however, I do believe it was one or two years before he gave up the idea of dribbling cards.

12

RELEASE VALVE

- *Shaving Cream*
- *Hide-and-Go-Seek in the House*
- *Drive-Through Car Washes*
- *Playing Ball in the House*
- *Blanket Sliding*
- *Ice Cubes*
- *Water Balloons*
- *Socks in a Sock*
- *Haircuts*
- *Making Bubbles*

Adults experience tension, failure, and anxiety now and then, but children, with all the rules, setbacks, and discipline they encounter, often rack up frustration, hour to hour.

No one questions the need for tension to be dissipated through some form of safety valve. Adults tend to hold it in or let it out in a socially acceptable way, but children aren't as well equipped. They generally release their tension, spontaneously and uncontrolled, which does have *some* mental health benefits. Unfortunately, though, their tension relief often takes the form of such unpleasant behavior as hitting a sibling, kicking the dog, drawing on walls, yelling at parents, pounding the floors, throwing things, and so on.

The result doesn't have to be this way though as there are many activities to siphon off the negative energy by positive means.

Moreover, since you have the option of participating in many of these diversions with your children, you may also find less need to visit your local mental health professional.

. . . There before me was a winter wonderland.

91. Shaving Cream   *"Winter Already?"*

Watch out, Picasso. Move over, Dali. Tough luck, Michelangelo. A new art form has emerged that just plain "cleans up." The great outdoors is its canvas. No boundaries, rules, or standards exist. It's pure free association. To initiate this artistry, issue one can of regulation shaving cream to your children and point them in the direction of the door. Better yet, escort them *out* the door, and lock it behind you. This is not an indoor activity.

What happens next is limited only by your child's imagination and creativity. Apparently my children's imagination conjured up a vision of winter. The first time I turned them loose with their can of compressed fun, I went to another part of the house. Upon my return, I looked out the window, and there before me was a winter wonderland. The entire deck in the back of the house, and all the objects on it, were completely white, including the patio furniture, children's furniture, barbecue grill, windows, plant, and a good portion of the dog and smallest child. With my knowledge based only on incremental shaving usage, I was astounded so much material could have emerged from such a small can. My first reaction was: *Oh my God, what have I done!* After I collected my wits and inspected the mess, I realized the worst that could happen was that I might end up with a completely clean deck.

With that in mind, I pondered my predicament and came up with a solution. Part II of the project would be to issue one regulation hose with running water. Wow! One activity that spawned another. It just doesn't get any better than this.

No matter what the children create, you can count on one thing: With a creamy, gooey, messy, soft, fragrant commodity that keeps on coming at the will of your child, this activity will keep the children's attention for as long as just about anything can. As with all great ideas though, there is always a potential downside. You have to figure that eventually exploitation will take over, and the can of shaving cream will become the can of "CREAMY OOZE," and sell in toy stores for $8.95.

92. Blanket Sliding   *"From A to Z"*

Did you know you can take your kids on a magic carpet ride in the comfort of your own home? Well, it isn't exactly magic—nor is it a carpet—but then again no foreign language skills are required and no money must be exchanged. The prerequisites are only that you have a slippery floor (hardwood, vinyl, tile), and a blanket (wool, acrylic, cotton). And unless you have a carpet fetish or sleep only in sleeping bags, you should be able to qualify. To ensure the maximum enjoyment and safety, here is a five-step approach suggested for pulling the blanket:

1. Place child (A) on Blanket (B).

2. Ask child (A) (if old enough), to select button . . .
    (C) Roller coaster
    (D) Grand Prix racing
    (E) Snow sled
    . . . on parent (F) for desired fantasy effect.

3. Parent (F), on the basis of judgment and child (A) desire, to select rate of SPEED and equivalent posture for him or her. The choices are:
    (G) DELIBERATE—sit-up
    (H) SLOW—hands out
    (I) MEDIUM—hold on
    (J) FAST—prone and holding on
    (K) SWERVING—add bike helmet to (J)
    (L) OUT-OF-CONTROL—add elbow and knee pads to (K)

4. Choose heading, obstacle course, and final destination. Your choices are:
    (M)   Toward the TV or (N) toward the coffee table
    (O-X) Obstacle Courses (ten to chose from; create these yourself)
    (Y-Z)   Sofa (Y) or Recliner (Z) for parent (F) at activities end

5. Child (A) says, "Go! Go! Go!"

If you want to add even more excitement, place a number of pillows at a hairpin turn and initiate controlled spinouts. Enlist Mom's involvement to have races—assuming two children and two blankets—or to lift child in air during the ride, for magic-carpet-ride-effect.

As this activity continues on and on, largely because of your child's plea of "More, more!"—and pouting lower lip, when you breathlessly attempt to persuade your child otherwise—you realize you no longer have a need for your Nordic Track, StairMaster, or aerobic tapes. You also no longer need to polish the floors; however, I would check out the cost of blanket dry cleaning.

The conclusion of the activity generally coincides with parental collapse. Nevertheless, you can take solace that your appreciative child will cover you with Blanket (B) for a good night's sleep.

93. Socks in a Sock   *"Sock-it-to-me"*

When I tell you to "put a sock in it," I'm not suggesting inserting a woven foot covering into the orifice between your nose and chin for the purpose of silencing you. I am encouraging you to place a rolled-up pair of socks into the end of a single sock, to form a device, I will call a Sock-it-to-me. This innocuous device has a number of uses, beyond the job of keeping your feet warm and dry.

PROTECT YOUR YOUNGEST CHILD FROM THE OLDEST CHILD: Children as well as adults require an appropriate outlet to vent frustrations. Beating up on a sibling, kicking a hole in the wall, or yelling at Mom doesn't quite qualify as appropriate. When your oldest child wants to take a bite out of your youngest child, furnish the Sock-it-to-me to help him or her channel anger. Instruct your child to beat it against the bed or floor, while expressing anger verbally, to help dissipate the frustration. (You could instruct your child to count to 10 instead, but that approach seems only to improve number learning.)

YOU DON'T HAVE TO WORRY ABOUT THE SCHOOL BULLY: The Sock-it-to-me is a safe way to expose your children to the art of defending themselves. You take one, and give one to your child. Swing away, ward off blows, and mix it up. The children will get the feel of what it is like to be the target of an aggressor, and perhaps they will fare better, if they get picked on.

MAKE THEM AN OLYMPIC FENCING HOPEFUL: Pair your children off with friends, or yourself, and go at it. The kids have to think offensively and defensively, simultaneously. They have to develop their body control, reflexes, and coordination. Moreover, you don't have to worry about jabs, pokes, or accidental skewering that might result from fencing, just some good *socks* to the torso.

KEEP THE HEART MUSCLE HAPPY AND FIT: Here is an aerobic game. Attire yourself in dark clothing and roll your Sock-it-to-mes in flour. Swing away, and dodge, duck, laugh, and chase. Respiration and pulse rate will move up at a steady clip. When the dusty white cloud clears, the one with the darker clothing wins.

If all the advantages of a sock-it-to-me aren't beneficial enough, consider this: The three-sock game takes advantage of those lone socks that have lost their mates in the black hole of the dryer.

94. Hide-and-Go-Seek in the House   *"Laughs a Minute"*

"Go hide. I'll count to 100 and then come looking for you," I claimed.

> "ONE, TWO." Let's see what's on TV. No. *(select)* No. *(select)* They're still in reruns?
> "EIGHT, NINE." Nothing on. Maybe I'll go make a sandwich. Bread, mayo, knife . . .
> "SIXTEEN, SEVENTEEN—I'M ALMOST TO ONE HUNDRED." Chips, milk . . .
> "TWENTY-SIX, TWENTY-SEVEN." Think I'll sit in the easy chair and read a magazine.
> "FORTY-ONE." Let's see. Oh, look Laughter is the Best Medicine. My favorite . . .
> "FIFTY-SIX, FIFTY-SEVEN." Yummm, good sandwich . . .
> "I'M JUST ABOUT THERE. YOU BETTER BE HIDDEN." Need to clip these darn nails . . .
> "SEVENTY-EIGHT, SEVENTY-NINE." Clip. Clip. Clip . . .
> "EIGHTY-SEVEN." Oh look, a ball game's on television!
> "TWENTY-SIX, TWENTY-SEVEN . . . . "

OK, you're right, it is a dirty trick, however, I only did it *one* time. No doubt I was exhausted and just didn't have the energy to play. Actually, I really enjoy the game. One of its more interesting aspects is the variety of laughter that erupts from my children when we're playing. Here are nine examples and the kind of LAUGHTER produced:

1. I hide and scare them by jumping toward them and blurting out, "Boo!" (HYSTERICAL)

2. I hide and make a short, sharp, noise to the degree they hear it, but can't tell where the sound is coming from. (NERVOUS)

3. They hide, and I talk loudly about how hard they are to find. (SUPPRESSED)

4. They hide, and I sneak up and shriek, "There you are!" (FRIGHTENED)

5. I hide, then move to a place where I know they have already looked and let them find me. I then convince them I have been there all along. (FRUSTRATED)

6. I hide in the bathroom, flush the toilet, then move somewhere else. (NERVOUS)

7. When I hide behind the easy chair, I peer up over it so they eventually see me from the nose up. (FRIGHTENED)

8. I hide and then throw a ball across the room as a diversion. They run to where it lands. (NERVOUS)

9. When I'm tired of playing, I go hide in the car. When my children can't find me, they go to Mom who is instructed to tell them, "When Daddy gets tired, he disappears into thin air and wakes up in a daze on the floor of the car." When they find me, they always tell me we should stop playing until I feel better. (SUBDUED)

Yes, I know—another dirty trick.

95. Ice Cubes *"The Labor Connection"*

Life is full of mysteries. Many may never be solved; Stonehenge, the pyramids, my children's craving for ice cubes. Well, I'm exaggerating a little. The first two might be solved, someday.

It is a rare occasion when my children aren't pirating ice cubes from my glass of iced tea. If you have any doubt, look in my mouth and see for yourself. "Ahhhhhh." Those ground-down molars got that way from breaking down large ice cubes into smaller ice bits, so the children could fit them in their mouths.

One day I saw the light. With necessity being the mother of invention, I discovered a way to save my teeth. I purchased a new refrigerator with an "ice mutilation" feature. I also realized that ice cubes don't *have* to spend time in a drink prior to being used for other means. So now, when the ice cube urge hits the children, I fill plastic cups with crushed ice, sit back down, and enjoy my iced tea—intact.

The children take the ice and chomp it, chew it, suck it, and melt it. They slide it, smash it, throw it, and down-each-other's-shirt it.

Ice cubes are so innocuous, yet amazingly the children never tire of their pleasure. Where does this allure of ice come from? Here are some possible explanations; although it's just speculation on my part.

1. Ice-play is a way to siphon off excess energy.
2. Unknown to science, in the freezing process ice takes on a vitamin or mineral essential for growth.
3. Children see ice turning to water as magical.
4. Children need to teethe, even for their permanent teeth.
5. Ice is a reminder of playful days in the snow.
6. Ice-play releases tension derived from the build up of . . . (no, too early for that).

Oh, I think I know why ice is so appealing to children. When my wife was in labor, the only nourishment she was allowed was ice chips! (Psych 101 sure comes in handy, sometimes.)

96. Haircuts   *"Just a Few Spins"*

Opie Taylor. Beaver Cleaver. Chip Douglas. The early family sitcom episodes that particularly stick in my mind are the ones where these fictional little boys got their haircuts. Nothing is more precious than a vulnerable little boy sitting still—a situation completely contradictory to his nature—while a person he doesn't know, wielding a sharp object, transforms him from a scruffy little boy into a clean-cut young man.

No doubt when your little boy had his first haircut, you cranked up the video camera, clicked at will on the still camera, and saved a lock of hair in an envelope. When the smock was pulled away, you shed a tear, because you weren't prepared for what you saw. You came in with your baby, but would have to leave with your little boy.

Time moves on, and haircuts become routine, but the experience can continue to be a delightful family adventure. Here's how to make it so. Set up consecutive appointments for the whole family, with your steady stylist. Many, as a smart business practice, will do your child's hair for free. Journey to the salon, but before entering the establishment, read your child the following 10 guidelines I have prepared, to enhance the experience.

1. BYPASS THE LOUNGE AREA. The waiting customers, ostensibly reading magazines, are so anxious about their impending hair experience, that you'll just make them crazier. Besides, you won't understand the magazines, anyway.

2. Go right for an EMPTY STYLIST'S CHAIR to take a few spins and make it go up and down, before someone tells you not to.

3. INGRATIATE YOURSELF with the stylists and clientele. This act will make whatever you want to do there later, much easier to get away with.

4. FIND A BROOM and sweep up, and around, all the discarded hair on the floor.

5. Place your head under the CONE-HEAD DRYERS and pretend to be an alien.

6. Observe the clients GET SHAMPOOED. (Don't look up their noses, though.)

7. Commandeer the electric clippers, and SHAVE THE HAIR off the back of Dad's hand.

8. Play with the yet-to-be-used TIN FOIL, SPONGES, AND CURLERS.

9. When it's your turn in the chair, INSTRUCT the stylist, "Just a little off the top, no mousse, and don't forget to clean up the hair down my neck."

10. As you are leaving and the receptionist gushes to your parents, "Your child is so cute, I'd just love to take him home," GRAB ONTO MOM, before she accepts the invitation.

97. Drive-Through Car Washes   *"A Fine Line"*

Sunday afternoon had arrived. A rare moment was before us because no individual commitments or activities were on the agenda. That meant the whole family could be together. To take advantage of this infrequent opportunity, we planned a nice Sunday outing.

All of us piled into the car prepared for our excursion, until we noticed a fuel problem. We had *too much*. Consequently we drove around aimlessly until the fuel level was low enough to go on our intended outing: A free drive-through car wash with a gas fill up.

The children had been begging to go there all week. (How can intelligent parents question their children's desire to do something easy, free, and not harmful to the teeth?) Going through the car wash was once a traumatic experience for them, but no more. The adventure has crossed over from being scary to being thrilling. Evidently, a fine line exists between fear and excitement.

With the car filled up with gas, we pulled into the "launch pad" as the blinking red light warned us to stop. Like space shuttle astronauts during countdown, we had the feeling there was no turning back.

We blasted off, despite warnings from Mission Control of menacing weather. The soap spewed down on us like a blizzard, and the water gushed like a downpour. The motors rumbled, and brushes spun like tornadoes. The dryer blasted like a desert wind storm. With each succeeding stage, the children's eyes grew larger. (Do the Disney folks know about this?)

We finally got through the bad weather and were given the green light for re-entry. We broke into the sunshine and negotiated a smooth landing. A nervous sigh of relief filled the cabin.

Like the astronauts who, after a landing, saunter around the craft marveling at how well it held up, the children scampered out and marveled at the cleanliness of our vehicle. They were proud and relieved they survived the mission.

Does the novelty of this amusement ever wear off for the children? Apparently not, because whenever my children enter the car, the first thing they do is eye the fuel gauge. If I have to refuse their requests to go to the car wash, they counter, "Can we go watch other cars drive through?"

My advice to you is this: Let them know who's the boss . . . no, inform them that what you say . . . no, state that you have had enough of . . . heck, take a box of crackers along; you're likely to get hungry.

98. Water Balloons   *"Icon for Fun"*

We associate brightly colored balloons with parties, celebrations, circuses, and fairs; just about any occasion where people are gathered to have a good time. (You just don't see too many balloons at funerals.) A balloon is an icon for fun.

If you combine balloons with the universal amusement for children, water (baths, pools, sprinklers, hoses, rain, squirt guns, and so on), then it's logical you should get twice the pleasure that you would get from either one by itself. And from what I have observed, I believe you do.

As I watch my youngest child carrying around the quivering, wobbling, jiggling sphere and laughing hysterically, I realize that the mere anticipation of it breaking is half the fun. When it breaks, it doesn't just break, it disintegrates. "YES!" my child shouts. When the balloon discharges, I imagine some of the frustrations do, too. Could such entertainment replace destructive behavior? Possibly.

To give you a flavor for this amusement, here are the Top 12 statements Dad makes while observing, or participating in the frivolity.

1.   "You can put one in your shirt, but be prepared to get wet."
2.   "Just remember, if you throw one at me, I can throw one at you."
3.   "I don't know. Roll it down the driveway and *see* if it will break."
4.   *"I wouldn't throw it at Mommy when she opens the front door, but you can."* *
5.   "OK. Get ready. Here it comes. Swing!"
6.   "That's the hundredth time you've run over one with your bike."
7.   "OK. Take one more step back and throw it to me again."
8.   "Break it with a ball? OK then, take the ball and stand behind this line."
9.   "Good shot! Right in the middle of the wagon."
10. "If I try to fill it up any more, it will explode in my face!"
11. "That's the farthest so far! Look at the splash mark!"
12. "Sure, it will work. Put a small hole in it, and you can squirt water forever."

* NOTE: Since this writing, I was forced to install a peephole in the front door, reducing this list to eleven.

99. Making Bubbles   *"Phenomenon of Relevance"*

A soap bubble manufactured by a child might very well hold the key to a scientific discovery that benefits mankind or cures a deadly disease. Consider this: A child, without giving it a second thought, can repeatedly produce a perfectly formed, ever-so-tenuously thin sphere, just by dipping a wand in a plastic bottle and blowing. An object formed so mysteriously, then living its life and vanishing all within the span of a few seconds, must be regarded as a phenomenon of great relevance.

Then again, maybe my interpretation gives bubbles a little more significance than you would prefer. Fine. Will you consider the notion that the bubble is a metaphor for fun and good times? How about these: Lawrence Welk and his bubble machine; a bubble dancer; Bubbles the Clown; Glinda the Good Witch of the North's bubble; bathtub bubbles; a bubble-gum bubble; Bubbles the whale; ocean bubbles; champagne bubbles; soft drink bubbles; soap bubbles; bubbly people; and so on.

OK, maybe this characterization still holds less significance than you were willing to ascribe to this orb. Well then, how about all the fun your children can have with soapy water and a wand? Yeah, I thought so.

Here are 10 bubbly pastimes for your children that *are* significant:

1. Who can make the most bubbles?
2. Whose bubble goes the farthest?
3. Whose bubble lasts the longest?
4. Who can make the biggest bubble?
5. How long can you make a bubble last on your hand?
6. Would you like to chase and pop the floating bubbles?
7. Who can make the smallest bubble?
8. Who can make a bubble float into a trash can?
9. Can you name all the colors swirling on the bubbles?
10. Who wants to observe the flight and serenity of the bubbles?

Then again, bubbles aren't *all* fun and games. I'm sure at some time, someone has burst your bubble.

Shelbyville-Shelby County
Public Library

100. Playing Ball in the House   *"No Storm Drains"*

I believe I began to notice the phenomenon as my kids became increasingly mobile. Balls of all different sizes and colors mysteriously appeared in a seemingly random fashion and multiplied all over the house. Their multiplication was mysterious, because I didn't recall buying most of them or receiving them as gifts. I deduced they were a private bunch and preferred the cozy climate of the house, because of their locations in corners, closets, behind chairs, and under beds.

Of course, children can't "let sleeping balls lie," so before long, ball playing in the house became a regular occurrence, much to the displeasure of Mom, who with the knowledge that if the perfect Brady and Cleaver families couldn't escape the hazards of ball playing in their houses, how could we?

The kids have so much fun playing ball, how could I deny them? Besides, I like to play, too. The wife is still a hold out, preferring to let basic common sense prevail. I figure, if it's good enough for model sitcom families, then why shouldn't it be good enough for us?

Generally, the beach ball is our ball of choice, given the "accident waiting to happen" scenario. Here are some games that have evolved in our home, but you can create your own games, too.

1. Free-form volleyball
2. Dodge ball
3. Soccer
4. Croquet (legs as wickets)
5. Catch
6. Ball over the couch (throw ball blindly over the couch to hit person on other side)
7. Circus seal (rolling and balancing on it)
8. Marco Polo dodge ball (try to hit target with eyes closed)

When the ball gets perilously close to small, breakable, valuable, or sentimental objects (dust collectors), we hear Mom warn, "What did I say about ball playing in the house?" We freeze and look at each other—decide the answer probably hasn't changed—remember there wasn't retribution the last time we ignored her, and continue with our game. It's just too hard to give up a game where you never get rained out, and you can't lose the ball down the storm drain.

13

POSITIVE REINFORCEMENT

• One Hundred Ways to Give Praise

If you remember nothing else from Psychology 101, other than the results of the work B. F. Skinner did with his pigeons, then the class was well worth your while. Skinner showed:

BEHAVIORAL CHANGE IS BEST ACCOMPLISHED

THROUGH POSITIVE REINFORCEMENT

What this finding means to us as parents is this: We should pat our children on the back, instead of spanking them on the bottom. We should give them a wink, instead of a scowl. We should tell them "good job," instead of "bad job." Simply put, our focus should be on reinforcing the good behavior, to achieve the results we want.

Put yourself in your child's place by comparing it to your job. Which statement from your boss would motivate you to do a better job? "You're doing a great job, keep up the good work," or "This work is very poor, certainly not up to our standards." True, the latter might scare you, and change your behavior in the short term, but in the long run, the positive statement will have the most impact.

Think about how often you focus on the bad behavior versus the good behavior with your children. How many times do you hand out a "bad boy" or "bad girl" for every "atta boy" and "atta girl?" Is the ratio 5 to 1, 10 to 1, possibly 20 to1?

Somewhere, sometime, somehow, we have mixed up and turned around our parental feedback, afraid we might spoil our children. Certainly we need to discipline children at times, but most certainly and more often, we need to reward them.

. . . A long way to reaping windfall profits.

101. One Hundred Ways to Give Praise *"REAP Vitamin"*

1. REASSURE to keep children going.
2. ENCOURAGE to get them started.
3. APPLAUD to bolster their self-esteem.
4. PRAISE to make everything seem worthwhile.

You can REAP the full potential of your children by investing very little. The following 100 "words," *touches*, and GESTURES will go a long way to reaping windfall profits. Based on providing one a day, here is a three-month plus supply of REAP vitamins to get you started:

"Good Job" ✦ "You Can Do It" ✦ A WINK ✦ "Top Notch" ✦ "Don't Worry" ✦ A THUMBS-UP ✦ "A plus" ✦ "Best I've Seen" ✦ "Excellent" ✦ "Tough It Out" ✦ "Trust Me" ✦ *A Squeeze on the Knee* ✦ "Bravo" ✦ FIST IN THE AIR ✦ "All Right!" ✦ "You Did That!" ✦ A NOD OF THE HEAD ✦ "Keep It Going" ✦ "Way to Go" ✦ "Who Taught You That?" ✦ "Love It" ✦ "Great" ✦ "Nice Work" ✦ *Hold a Child's Hand* ✦ "Superb" ✦ "To the Top" ✦ "You'll Get 'em Next Time" ✦ "That's 110 Percent" ✦ "Nothing Ventured Nothing Gained" ✦ *Lift a Child Up* ✦ "Baffo!" ✦ "I Couldn't Have Done It Better" ✦ *Arm Around Shoulder* ✦ "Way to Go" ✦ AN OK SIGN ✦ "Can't Beat That" ✦ "Amazing" ✦ "Have Fun" ✦ *A Pat on the back* ✦ "Yes!" ✦ A SMILE ✦ "Go for It" ✦ A NOSE WIGGLE ✦ "Good Job" ✦ *A Hand Shake* ✦ "Good Girl (Boy)" ✦ "Go Get 'em" ✦ *A Hug* ✦ "You're the Best" ✦ "You're #1" ✦ "I'll Be There" ✦ ARMS OPEN ✦ "Wow!" ✦ *Muss Up Hair* ✦ A SALUTE ✦ "Fantastic!" ✦ "Wonderful" ✦ *A Low Five* ✦ "Hot Dog" ✦ "Magnificent Effort" ✦ *Swing the Child Around* ✦ "Cool" ✦ "Extraordinary" ✦ *A Pat on the Bottom* ✦ "Socko" ✦ "That's All Right" ✦ *A Neck Squeeze* ✦ "Relax" ✦ *Hoist on shoulders* ✦ "Grab for the Gusto" ✦ *A Gentle Shake* ✦ "Be the Best" ✦ *Stroke Hair* ✦ "No Sweat" ✦ "That's the Ticket" ✦ "Too Good" ✦ "Perfect" ✦ "Good Try" ✦ "You're a Winner" ✦ "Never Quit" ✦ "Don't Give Up" ✦ "Almost!" ✦ *A Pat on the Cheek* ✦ "Marvelous" ✦ "Dynamite" ✦ "Hooray" ✦ "Terrific" ✦ *Hands on Shoulders* ✦ "You're on Target" ✦ "Awesome" ✦ "You Made My Day" ✦ *A high five* ✦ "That's Your Niche" ✦ "Bingo" ✦ *A kiss* ✦ A HAND CLAP ✦ "Big Improvement" ✦ "Great Progress" ✦ "V" FOR VICTORY ✦ "I'm Proud to Be Your Dad"

CONCLUSION

157,000 Hours

There is no formal education to obtain or tests to pass. There is no apprenticeship to complete or rehearsal to attend. There is no oath to take or license to get. There is no instruction book to study or equipment to aid you. *This* is the foundation you will build on, for unarguably the most important endeavor you will execute in your lifetime—parenting. This shocking paradox makes the mindset and path you take from day one critical to your success. For at least the next 18 years—6,570 days—157,000 plus hours—you will be shaping a human life.

There are a few essential messages I want every reader to come away with. The first is that parenting doesn't have to be an overwhelming undertaking; the most complex tasks are often addressed with simple solutions. Second, a critical key to parenting rests with your children; follow and trust their instincts. Third, you are the lock, so allow your children "to turn the key" in you often; play an integrated and active role. Last, you will reap what you sow; your enrichment will be directly proportional to your child's.

Not a Dress Rehearsal

Remember, life is not a dress rehearsal. This is your one and only chance to parent your children. Time never goes backwards. Make the most of it and you'll have no regrets. Do more than merely move your children along, satisfying their basic needs of safety, shelter, and schooling for 18 years. Be a performer in the main act. Let it all hang out.

Think about one more thing. Unless you have a statue erected in your honor, or a stadium named after you, your face in an ageless movie, or a product carrying your name, you will be immortalized mostly through your children. If not for them, much of your memory and influence would end with your final breath. So, how do you want to be remembered? What you do with your children will determine how *you* live on forever.

Creased, Dog-Eared, and Jelly-Stained

I hope the book you are holding is creased, dog-eared, and jelly-stained. If it is, then I know you have enjoyed many of the proverbial boxes presented, discovered many of your own, and are on your way to a successful and rewarding parenting journey.

ABOUT THE AUTHOR

Rex Bowlby holds a B. A. in Psychology from the University of California, Santa Barbara, and an M. S. in Management and Organizational Dynamics, from the University of La Verne. A contributor to *Modern Dad* magazine, he has parented for over 96,000 hours so far. He lives with his wife and two boys in Atlanta, Georgia, and is always on the lookout for the next box.

INDEX

INDEX